Genealogy Of The Meyer Family

Henry Meyer

GENEALOGY

OF THE

MEYER FAMILY.

BY

HENRY MEYER.

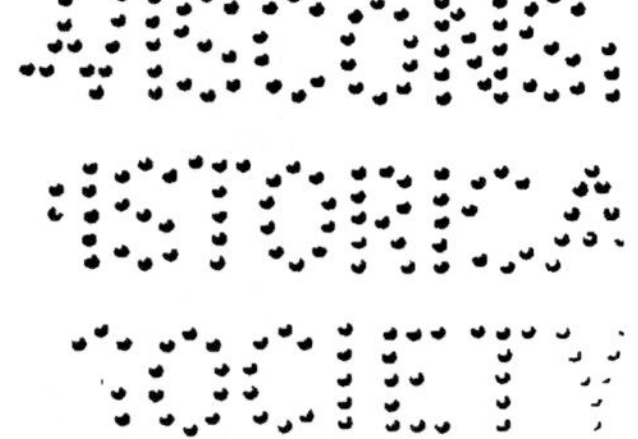

1890.

PRINTED BY LAUER & MATTILL, CLEVELAND, O.

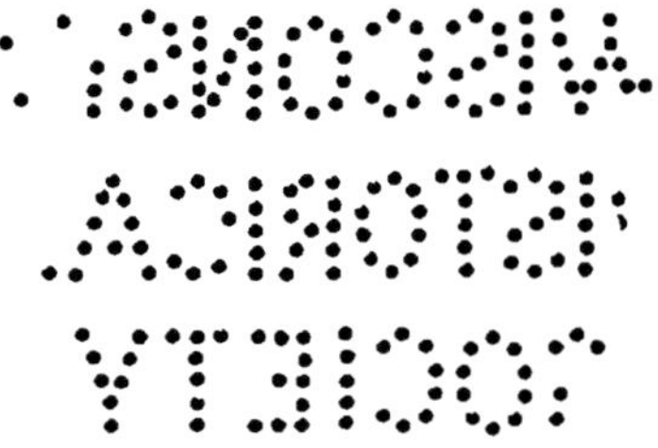

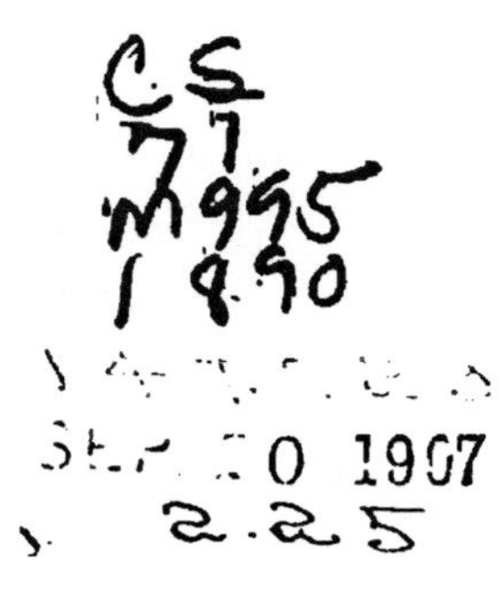

INDEX.

PREFACE.

Originally these sketches and genealogies of the Meyer family were prepared, not for publication, but for the author's own use and satisfaction. There are many facts and anecdotes in the unwritten history of the old stock of Meyers, which are rapidly passing into oblivion, and it was considered a duty incumbent upon some one to make a record of them somewhere while a portion at least was still accessible. At the solicitation of many of the Meyer connection, however, the author has changed his original purpose as to the publication of the sketches, and they were prepared for the printer, thus giving an opportunity to the numerous descendants of the Meyer family to enlarge, it is hoped, their fund of knowledge in relation to their kin and ancestors. But the step was not taken without some reluctance, for the writer is conscious of the fact that in the absence of records, no accurate and complete history of events, some of which occurred almost two hundred years ago, could now be prepared. It is certainly to be regretted, that some representative of the family did not address himself to the task of writing the history of his ancestors at an earlier date, for nearly all that is known on the subject now is merely tradition, and much has already been lost which would be of peculiar interest, if preserved, to a numerous train of descendants. Many dates can be given approximately only, and traditions in the different branches of the family in regard to the same event do not always correspond. It may be proper to say, however, that considerable pains were taken to sift everything carefully, and reject what was doubtful, so that the reader may rely on the statements presented as being in general correct. It would have added to the interest and value of this book if more of the earlier dates, many of which are now unfortunately lost, could have been supplied; special efforts were made to secure all the dates and items of interest in relation to the old stock of the family, rather than give minute details concerning later generations. The design has been to present but a brief work. To extend the genealogies beyond the fifth (American) generation would make this work quite extensive. The author considers his duty at least partially discharged in furnishing a concise statement of his subject, which may form a trunk upon which branches of individual families may easily be grafted by future genealogists.

The greater portion of the material for this book was collected in 1882 and 1883, but some additions have been made up to the time of publication, January, 1890; these latter are accompanied by their proper dates.

Since these sketches were prepared originally for the benefit of his own family and near relatives the writer made frequent use of the pronoun "I" and the terms "uncle", "parents", "cousins", to avoid in some degree the obscurity and confusion incident on the constant recurrence of the same names in the succession of generations. It was thought proper to retain this style in this work.

A large part of the information contained in these pages was obtained from representatives of the different branches of the family through correspondence, and credit is usually given for such contributions at the proper place. But the author is under special obligations to Hon. Jacob G. Meyer, Aaronsburg, Pa.; Maj. John Meyer and Henry Meyer (dec'd), Rebersburg, Pa.; Frederick C. Meyer, Freeburg, Pa., and Mrs. Amanda Steese, Lake, O., for valuable assistance rendered.

HENRY MEYER.

Rebersburg, Pa., January, 1890.

EARLY HISTORY

OF

THE MEYER SETTLEMENT IN AMERICA.

THE MEYERS seem to have been quite numerous in some parts of Germany. This may be inferred from the large number that have annually emigrated to this country from a very early period of its settlement by Europeans up to the present. It is not pretended that all the individuals of this name are blood relations, for in some sections it is almost as universal as the surname Smith or Miller. Before the Great West was opened for settlement, Pennsylvania received probably more of these Meyer emigrants than any other state. The land records at Harrisburg, Pa., show that from 1733 to 1752 the Meyer name occurs about fifty times in connection with tracts of land taken up in Lancaster County, but among them some names appear several times, as the same person took up different tracts. A copy of the list is given in note below,[1] but its only value is to show that the Meyer immigrants were numerous in the early history of

1. *Note.*—These were tracts taken up in Lancaster County, but some are at present within the limits of Lebanon County, which was taken from Lancaster:

John Moyer,	100 acres,	Jan. 24, 1733.
John and Michael Meier,	550 "	Oct. 23, 1733.
Hans Meier,	100 "	Feb. 28, 1734.
John Moyer,	250 "	April 8, 1734.
Martain Maier,	200 "	" 22, 1734.
Dannis Meier,	150 "	Aug. 13, 1734.

Pennsylvania. Which of these names belonged to our ancestors and relatives can not now be ascertained.

It might be here stated, since the name *Meyer* is spelled in different ways by different members of this numerous family, that among the emigrant ship lists on file at Harrisburg, Pa., it is never found written *Moyer;* most frequently it is written Meyer. So also in old deeds and other papers signed a hundred or a hundred and fifty years ago the name is always spelled Meyer or Mayer. However, in the records at Harrisburg and other places, where clerks and officials wrote the name, we see it written in many different ways—Meyer, Myer, Meyers, Myers, Mire, Meier, Meir, Mayer, Moyer. Of course our ancestors wrote German and spelled their name Meyer, which properly translated is *Meyer*, and this form has been adopted for this work.

Our ancestor Meyer who settled in this country came from the Palatinate, Prussia. After extensive inquiries among his descendants I have failed to ascertain his christian name. My father (Henry Meyer, born 1795, died 1881) thought it was *Christopher*. Hon. Jacob G. Meyer, Aaronsburg, Pa., thinks so too. Several others have this impression, but none know positively. My opinion is that his name was Henry; reasons for which will be given in another place. Little is

---

Michael Meier,	50 acres,	May 24, 1735.
Jacob Meyer,	50 "	Jan. 2, 1737.
Henry Meyer,	200 "	" 9, 1737.
Henry Meier,	150 "	June 17, 1737.
Michael Moyer,	487 "	Nov. 2, 1737.
Jacob Meyer,	200 "	" 23, 1737.
Christopher Meyer,	200 "	March 30, 1738.
Elias Mayer,	200 "	June 7, 1738.
Henry Moyer,	300 "	Sept. 29, 1738.
Jacob Meyer,	200 "	Oct. 12, 1738.
George Moyer,	150 "	" 18, 1738.

known about this Meyer while in this country, and still less about his history before he came across. Many genealogies are lost in the Atlantic Ocean. Maj. John Meyer, Rebersburg, Pa., states, he often heard his uncle Philip Meyer (grandson of the Meyer from Germany) say that two brothers came with our ancestor across from the old country, and that one of them returned to his home because he did not like this country, while the other went to the Carolinas in quest of a warmer climate. Father used to say that two daughters of our ancestor moved to one of the Carolina states, and it is quite probable that some male relative had preceded them. Samuel Meyer, Iowa, son of the Philip above mentioned, says that he was always told "that three brothers came together, two of whom settled in Pennsylvania, the other left there and was never heard from." Two separate tracts of land were taken up at the old Meyer settlement, Mühlbach, Lebanon County, Pa., one by John Meyer and the other by Henry Meyer, adjoining, and the probability is that these were brothers and that one of them was our ancestor. This subject will again be referred to in another place. In reference to the question whether one of those brothers above mentioned moved to Carolina (South Carolina), it is reliably stated that Meyer relatives from that section used to come

---

Hans Jacob Moyer,	100 acres,	Nov. 16, 1738.
John Meyer,	100 "	Oct. 25. 1739.
Michael Moyer,	188 "	July 18, 1741.
Jacob Mayer,	100 "	Feb. 28, 1742.
Michael Moyer,	150 "	July 13, 1742.
Nicholas Mayer,	100 "	Aug. 19, 1742.
Vincent Moyer,	50 "	Oct. 6, 1742.
John Moyer,	100 "	" 19, 1743.
John Meier,	100 "	" 21, 1743.
Stoffel Moyer,	200 "	Dec. 22, 1743.
John Meier,	50 "	Oct. 11, 1744.

to the old Mühlbach homestead, and visited also Michael Meyer, who moved to Ohio.

Our ancestor, Mr. Meyer, settled permanently at the beautiful spring or source of the small stream known by the name *Mühlbach* (Mill Creek), Lancaster County, Pa., but now in the south-eastern part of Lebanon County, as the latter was taken from the former. About this question there can be no doubt. It is a tradition in different branches of the Meyer family. I often heard father repeat the story how his great-grandfather and great-grandmother arrived at that Spring and began life anew in the new country; and his circumstantial account of the event agrees substantially with versions given by Hon. Jacob G. Meyer, Maj. John Meyer, Mrs. Nancy (Meyer) Kryder and others. This spring is in Mill Creek township near the line between this and Heidleberg township (Mill Creek was taken from Heidleberg). As already stated, this spring is the source of the Mühlbach creek, a small stream which flows east and northeast into the historic Tulpehocken. I visited the place several times during the Spring and Summer of 1883, and a brief description of the old homestead and its neighborhood may not be inappropriate.

Getting off the train at Sheridan Station, L. V. R. R., one

'Christian Moyer,	100 acres,	Jan. 16, 1746.
John Moyer,	100 "	" 16, 1746.
Fred. Moyer,	100 "	Oct. 28, 1746.
Jacob Moyer,	160 "	" 14, 1747.
George Moyer,	100 "	Nov. 19, 1748.
John Mayer,	30 "	" 21, 1748.
Jacob Moyer,	100 "	Feb. 2, 1749.
Jacob Meyer,	100 "	March 15, 1749.
Henry Mayer,	50 "	Aug. 17, 1749.
Christopher Meyer,	100 "	Oct. 9, 1749.
Jacob Myer,	150 "	Nov. 15, 1749.

travels in a south-western direction through a fine farming region part way through beautiful meadows along the Mühlbach, a distance of about three miles to reach the spring. The Mühlbach post village, where stands the old Lutheran and Reformed Church in the old cemetery, in which are buried many of the first Meyer settlers, is passed within a mile of the spring. This is an old country, historic; it was settled as early as the year 1720. One will pass many buildings over a hundred years old. There are yet standing solid, fortress-like stone houses, which were constructed with a view of defense against attacks from the Indians, and several did good service in that way.

I found a beautiful spring at the old homestead supplying a small stream, which still is the abode of fine trout. It is limestone water. George Meyer of Dauphin, who was raised there, says that it discharges about one-fourth less water than formerly. He says they used to clean it once a year. I viewed the spot with peculiar interest, and the oft repeated traditions I had heard from my childhood came back vividly to my mind. I may have been standing on the very spot where our great-great-grandmother had prostrated herself on the ground in grief and tears, when she and her husband tarried here under a tree from their long and weary wanderings, seeking a home in the wild forest of a strange country. No wonder that tears were shed. No house to shelter them

John Meyer,	100 acres,	April 11, 1750.
Philip Myer,	100 "	June 7, 1750.
Hans Moyer,	50 "	" 14, 1750.
Michael Meyer,	50 "	Dec. 8, 1750.
Jacob Meyer,	100 "	Aug. 6, 1751.
Jacob Moyer,	50 "	Sept. 24, 1751.
Lawrence Myer,	50 "	March 23, 1752.
Jacob Moyer,	100 "	May 5, 1752.
Jacob Moyer,	50 "	" 14, 1752.

and their children; no furniture of any kind; but little, if any, food; they had nothing but an axe and a few indispensable articles which they carried in a bundle. Nothing but forest wherever they turned their eyes, and for all they knew hostile Indians might even then be prowling around them on the adjacent ridges. Their few neighbors were far off and equally poor, and as the poor woman contemplated their forlorn situation, it is no wonder that her mind should revisit the scences of her childhood-home across the wide, wide ocean. Yet it must have been a beautiful spot, and a more desirable location for their home could not have been found in that region. North of the spring is a considerable elevation and a slight one on the south still covered with woods, and between these flows the Mühlbach in an eastern direction for some distance, then bending its course north and north-east, receiving tributaries from a number of other fine springs all along until it empties into the Tulpehocken. The farm-house and barn are north of the spring. The house is the third on the place, and was preceded by a log-cabin which stood across the road, north of the present building. It was removed about the year 1840, and the material used in the construction of another house somewhere in the neighborhood, and was burned down afterward. But there used to be a small cabin quite close to the spring, which it is supposed was the first dwelling house on the place. Widow Meyer, who lives on the farm at present (1883), describes the cabin as having been about ten by twelve feet, one story high, containing one low door, two small windows, one of which had but two panes, and a chimney at one end of the room. It was moved down the run some fifty rods about the year 1858, enlarged, and is there this day.

A small stable affording room for one cow stood near by. The present buildings on the place are substantial; the house is of rough stones. Land there is worth from $150 to $175 per acre. The place has never been owned by any person except descendants of the Meyer who first settled on it.[1] My father used to say the old homestead was still owned by Meyers of the old stock. The genealogy of the Meyer families in that section will be given in its proper place.

The date of the arrival of Mr. Meyer in this country can be ascertained approximately only. He was without doubt one of the first settlers in the Mühlbach region, and from local histories it appears that the first white people located there about the year 1721–1723. "Among the early settlers on Mill Creek were Conrad Bissel, Joseph Shaeffer, Hans Meyer, Henry Hoehn and several Landises." "Conrad Bissel settled on Mühlbach in 1721. He and Stuntz built a house. They were soon joined by Isaac Von Barben, George Steifel and others." — *Rupp's Hist. Lancaster County.* In a recent history of Dauphin and Lebanon Counties by Dr. W. H. Egle, occurs the following: "Conrad Weiser, his wife and five children came from Schoharie, N. Y., in 1723, and settled at Mühlbach, afterward he moved to the present site of Womelsdorf. He was accompanied to Mühlbach by John Stump, Michael Meiser, John Noll, Michael Zeller, John Moore, Henry Moyer, Nicholas Lechner, John Grove and Christ. Seibert, all settled at Mühlbach." It will be observed that in the foregoing extracts we have the two names Henry Meyer and Hans (John) Meyer among the list of early settlers. There is a tradition that our ancestor did belong to Conrad Weiser's colony. Among the old papers of the Mühlbach Meyer homestead, I found a draft of 346¾ acres

---

1. *Note.*—The farm was divided years ago, and the eastern part, which contains the spring, passed into the hands of J. M. Zimmerman, Dec. 9, 1887.

of land taken up by Henry Meyer, Sept. 29, 1738; the adjoining tracts being owned by John Moore, J. Baker, Wendel Loutermilk, Ben Scheffer and John Moyer.[1] This undoubtedly is the draft of the original tract on which our ancestor located, and it shows that there were at that time two Meyers, Henry and John. While there is no positive proof, my opinion is that Henry was our ancestor, and that John was his brother. But the following facts which are handed down to us may perhaps be of more value in determining the time when Mr. Meyer brought his family to America. On their arrival at Mühlbach the family consisted of husband, wife and one or two children. John was the oldest *son* and must have been the child (or one of the two) brought from Germany. As near as can be ascertained he was born in 1719. It would, therefore, be probable that the family came to Mühlbach sometime during the period between the years 1721 and 1725.

It has been stated already that little is known of our ancestor's history while in this country, nor while still a resident of the Palatinate. The few facts that we have in our possession will, therefore, be the more interesting and should be carefully treasured, though of but little intrinsic value.

---

1. *Note.*—Among the taxables in Heidleberg township in the year following the separation of Berks from Lancaster, 1752, are found John Mire and Henry Mire. Six years later, John Myer is assessed 0£. 8s. 6d.; Henry Myer, 0£. 6s. 0d.; Isaac Meyer, 0£. 17s. 0d.—This Isaac Meyer, the founder of Meyerstown, Pa., was assassinated in a public house at Meyerstown, Pa., July 15, 1770. Some person shot him through a window after night. He was born June 4, 1730; lies buried in the old cemetery of the Tulpehocken Reformed Church. Isaac Meyer had been a Justice of the Peace; was prominent in his section. He was related in some way to the Mühlbach Meyers. Heister Clymer is a descendant.

Mr. Meyer served a term of seven years in the army in the old country, and with this fact is connected a romance, which, while not of great importance, may, nevertheless, be of sufficient interest to preserve. Before entering the army Mr. Meyer became engaged to a young lady who subsequently became his wife. But while serving his time in the army his girl fell in love with another fellow, which brought on a lovers' quarrel with her betrothed. Mr. Meyer pretended to be quite indifferent about his former sweetheart, and while passing her home in going to and coming from his work he whistled and sang and in other ways showed his indifference. She relented and sent for him, when a reconciliation took place. He was a fine singer, which it is said had its effect in changing the lady's feelings. They were married and ere many years came to America. Most of their little property they sold to pay part of their passage across the ocean. Several pigs and a few pieces of furniture was all they had.[1] They landed at New York, and after serving a time to pay the balance of their fare across the ocean, came to Philadelphia. Thence traveling on foot through the country, working a day or two occasionally to defray expenses, they finally arrived, while looking for a place to settle, at the beautiful spring in the forest, which seemed to have a strong attraction for Mr. Meyer, and he said, "Here we will stay." The bundles which they carried were unloaded under a large white oak tree, and the

---

1. *Note.*—George C. Meyer, Freeburg, Pa., gives the following version of this part of the story:—"Mr. Meyer had to make up a certain sum of money to pay his taxes, and he took his pigs to market to sell for that purpose. Meeting there some of his comrades, they repaired to a tavern, where the money was soon spent, and the taxes remained unpaid. Money and pigs gone, and being extremely poor, he became dissatisfied with his hard lot, and resolved to emigrate to America."

husband christened the stream *Mühlbach*, after the name of his native home in the old country. Their possessions were exceedingly limited, consisting of an axe, two tin plates, some clothing and a few other indispensable articles. It was sometime after harvest that the family arrived at the spring, about four o'clock in the afternoon of a certain day.[1]

When Mr. Meyer died, how old he was or where he is buried, are questions that will, perhaps, never be answered. It is probable that he and his wife lie buried in the cemetery of the old Mühlbach church, as that would have been the most convenient, and there are buried many of his descendants.[2] I visited the cemetery in company with Henry Meyer, Mühlbach, in the Spring of 1883, but found no tombstone with a record that might apply to him. Many graves have no markers, others have tombstones without inscriptions, and

---

1. *Note.*—I am indebted to Hon. Jacob G. Meyer and my father for most of the above facts. Father often made mention of the tin or pewter plates, and how his great-grandfather named the stream. Mrs. Nancy Kryder, Cedar Springs, Pa. (deceased), says the family had one child. That the parents located under a tree near the spring. That the wife sat on the ground and cried while the husband went to work with his axe making a clearing.

---

2. *Note.*—Among the Meyers buried at Mühlbach, the following have tombstones with inscriptions:—

Moyer, Catharine (wife of J. M.), born, Oct. 1747; died, Oct. 11, 1825. See page 25.

Moyer, Catharine (w. of J. M.), born, Oct. 15, 1789; died, May 9, 1852.

Moyer, John George, born, Sept. 7, 1783; died, Oct. 22, 1804. See page 28. (?)

Moyer, Johannes, died Dec. 11, 1786, aged 67 years. See page 22.

Meyer, Elizabeth (w. of J. G. M.), born, Jan. 30, 1779; died, April 7, 1855.

Meyer, John George, born, Oct. 13, 1774; died, Oct. 21, 1826.

still others have inscriptions, but so much defaced and worn by the elements that they can not be deciphered. I also visited both the Lutheran and Reformed Churches at the Tulpehocken, and the old Reed's Church, farther east, and examined old church records and cemeteries, but found absolutely nothing that I thought could apply to our ancestor.

The Meyers about Mühlbach, who are the descendants of John, seem to know rather less about the early family history than those of their kin (descendants of Jacob and Christopher) who live at a distance. This is natural. Through their continuous residence at the old homestead or in its immediate vicinity, and their participation in later events there, they would be likely to lose interest in the incidents of its earlier history, and finally forget most of them ; while on the other hand, Jacob and his family and Christopher left the old home at a period when the story of its settlement was still green in their memories, and thus would be cherished by them and their descendants as precious relics of the old homestead.

As already stated, a large number of Meyers settled in this country, and in looking over the assessment list of the townships in the southern and eastern parts of Lebanon county, the name is found to occur quite frequently from the year 1752 to 1800. Of course their names appeared earlier, but the records of Lancaster county up to the date 1752 have been lost, I believe. Some of these names apply to the Mühlbach Meyers, and many others may have been relatives of them coming from the same section of the Palatinate. The Stouchsburg Meyers, Berks county, Pa., claim relationship with the Mühlbach Meyers, and there are some traits of resemblance, but their ancestor[1] came across just prior to the

---

1. *Note.*—Nicholas Meyer was the ancestor of this family, and came from the old country about the time of the Revolution. He was married before he came across, and had one son, Daniel. Nicholas

Revolutionary War. Them also I visited and "interviewed" in the Spring of 1883, and was very kindly entertained.

The rest of this sketch will now be devoted to the genealogy of the three families of John, Jacob and Christopher Meyer, and such items of history as have been collected and may seem appropriate. These are the only sons of the Meyer who came from Europe, that had issue. The facts of the following sketches were furnished by representatives of their respective branches of families, and are, no doubt, in the main, reliable. I took special care to verify traditions and statements in various ways before inserting them here, and in order to be on the safe side some items may have been rejected which should have been retained.

Several branches of families have not been traced down as far as could be desired, because of the difficulty encountered

---

was born about the year 1750, died about the year 1800. Daniel, his son, lived near Stouchsburg, Berks Co., Pa.; he died March 1850, aged about 66 years. Left eight *children*:—

I. JOHN, lived at Stouchsburg; had issue:—1. John, born April 1, 1830; lives at Stouchsburg; 2. Adam; 3. Levi, Stouchsburg; 4. Melinda, m. John Kintzell; 5. Isaac, proprietor of hotel and store, Stouchsburg; 6. Joshua; 7. Maria, m. W. Deck.

II. ELIZABETH.

III. SARAH.

IV. DANIEL.

V. CATHARINE.

VI. MARY.

VII. ISAAC.

VIII. SUSAN, married to George Fornwalt. Lives at Stouchsburg, Pa. She was born July 16, 1819. I visited her April 21, 1883, and received these facts from her. She says John Nicholas Meyer and Jacob Meyer (whoever *they* may have been) were cousins of her grandfather, Nicholas Meyer.

This family write their name *Moyer*.

in securing the necessary information. Dates of birth and death are usually given if known.

How many children the Germany Meyer had could not be ascertained definitely with regard to the daughters. Father used to say there were four sons and two daughters, the latter having both moved to the Carolinas. Mrs. Nancy Kryder, mentioned before, stated there was one daughter only, that she moved to one of the Carolinas, and was heard from only once after her removal thence.

Children of the Meyer who came from Germany.

John. See page 22.

Jacob. See page 34.

Michael. See page 129.

Christopher. See page 89.

Daughter (one or two). See page 129.

JOHN MEYER (son of the Meyer from Germany) owned the old homestead at the Mühlbach, and is said to have been the oldest son, but his sister (or sisters) may have been older. The probability is that he was born in Germany, and was the child (or one of the two) brought by the parents from the old country. Yet there is nothing certain about this. Letters of administration were granted to his "oldest son John" to settle up the estate, Dec. 22, 1786, and it is likely that he, the subject of this sketch, died but a short time previous. On a tombstone in the Mühlbach cemetery is this record: "Johannes Moyer, Died Dec. 11, 1786; aged 67 years." This record and the letters of administration granted eleven days later no doubt have reference to the same person. His wife's Christian name also is mentioned in the papers just alluded to, and was Anna Barbara. The names of his children are found on an old deed,[1] dated Dec. 3, 1788,

---

Note.—EXPLANATIONS.—The different *styles* or *forms* of numerals used throughout this book will distinguish the different generations of the persons with which they are connected. Calling the children of the Meyer who came from Germany the first generation, their children, or the second generation, will be distinguished thus: **I. II.** etc.; the third, I. II. etc.; the fourth, 1. 2. 3. etc. The names in brackets show the descent of the individual with which they are connected.

The reader may readily trace to its particular branch of the family any name found on any page of the book by remembering the above instructions.

---

1. *Note.*—DEED.—"Henry Moyer, wife Anna Engle:—Anna Margaret and husband Jacob Neff; Elizabeth and husband John Moore; Barbara and husband Ludwich Miller (the said Henry, Anna, Margaret, Elizabeth and Barbara being children of John Moyer, late of Heidleberg township, deceased) conveyed to John Moyer, eldest son of said John Moyer, deceased, etc. Dated Dec. 3, 1788, patented

found among the papers of the Mühlbach homestead. The younger brother Henry and the sisters sold their interest in their father's farm to their older brother John. This list must include all the children that had grown to maturity and were still living. If any had died before the sale of the farm the fact is not known. John's descendants can give but little information about him. George, of Dauphin, and Michael, from near Mühlbach, grandsons, and among the very last of that generation yet living, simply know that his name was John (Hans), that he owned the old Mühlbach homestead, and that he was in some way related to Christopher Meyer of Campbellstown, Lebanon County. From these meager facts, from information given by Mrs. Nancy Kryder, who was raised at her grandfather Christopher's place, at Campbellstown, Pa., from traditions remembered by Henry and John Meyer, Rebersburg, Pa., and from items discovered in old documents, I have been able to form a chain of evidence which leaves no doubt in my mind as to his location in the Meyer family. After the lapse of a few more years this fact could not have been established.

It is related that John, or "Hans," as he was more familiarly known by his relatives, was an excellent violinist. When visiting his friends it was not long until he would have handed him the violin, an almost indispensable piece of furniture in the Meyer homes of that period, and, after excusing himself a while, exhibiting his crooked, bony fingers and asking how they could expect one to play with

---

to John Moyer, March 3, 1759. See Book A, vol. 20, page 240. Recorded at Harrisburg, Pa. Book D, vol. 1, page 167.

Another deed among same papers:—John Meyer, and wife Anna Barbara, conveying tract of land to Henry Meyer, Dec. 8, 1767. Richard Tea had conveyed this to John Meyer, Jan. 27, 1755. Book F, 293, Heidleberg township.—I did not ascertain whether these deeds apply to the same tract.

such hands, he would tune the instrument and perform with wonderful ability. From time immemorial the Meyers have been noted singers, and nearly all the older stock could play the violin. They made their own instruments, and were, therefore, not very expensive. It was about the only musical instrument then in existence among the pioneer settlers, and, however rude in construction, it would answer the purpose of rasping sundry tunes for dancing!

John had five children as far as we know (see deed page 22), two sons and three daughters. About the latter no information was received. The descendants of John (the subject of this sketch,) are nearly all residing in Dauphin and Lebanon Counties; quite a number near Mühlbach.

List of Children.

John. *See* page 25.

Henry. *See* page 30.

Anna Margaret. *See* page 33.

Elizabeth. *See* page 33.

Barbara. *See* page 33.

I. JOHN (son of John, son of Gr. Meyer) was the eldest son of the family and was born March 3, 1745; died June 15, 1812. His wife Catharine, was born, Oct. 1747; died Oct. 11, 1825. Both are buried in the Mühlbach cemetery. His wife was a daughter of Alexander Schaeffer,[1] the founder of Schaefferstown, Lebanon County, Penna., and a sister of Anna Maria Schaeffer, who was married to Christopher Meyer of Campbellstown, Lebanon Co., Penna. John was a nephew of Christopher and great-grandfather Jacob Meyer. I have already stated in another place that he settled up his father's estate, and that he had purchased the old homestead from his brother and sisters. Michael, a grandson, states that John was a teamster in the Revolutionary War. These few facts were given by Michael (just named) and John of Mühlbach and George of Dauphin, Pa., all grandsons and very old men (1883).

There were seven children, four sons and three daughters:—

I. JOHN (John, John, Gr. Meyer) was married, first, to Lizzie Strickler, 2nd, to Christina Lise. He owned the old

---

1. *Note.*—Schaeffer was a native of the Palatinate, and came to America in 1740. He lived a while in Heidleberg township (Mühlbach), thence moved to the site of Schaefferstown. Was born Jan. 8, 1712; died April 12, 1786. Married first Eva Engle; issue:—

I. Henry.
II. Salina, m. Michael Hoke.
III. Anna Maria, m. Christopher Meyer.
IV. Catharine, m. John Meyer.
V. Margaret, m. John Bright.
VI. John, d. prior to 1787; left issue.
VII. Anna Eva, b. Apr. 27, 1753, died Jan. 2, 1790.
Alexander married a second time.

Dr. Wm. H. Egle's Hist. Dauphin & Lebanon.

Mühlbach home *after* his brother Michael. Died, May 9, 1851, aged seventy-two and one-half years about. Lies buried at the Mühlbach church.

ISSUE, FIRST WIFE—LIZZIE STRICKLER:

1. GEORGE, married, first Lizzie Becker, second, Leah Stoucher. He was born in 1804 at Mühlbach and was raised there. At present (1883) he lives at Dauphin, north of Harrisburg, Pa., where his sons carry on a butcher shop. I visited him in the Spring of 1883 and received from him many facts in relation to the Meyers of his branch of the family. *Children:* Rebecca, married Ed. Ebach; John, dec'd, married Sarah Smith. (These were children of the first wife, Lizzie Becker.) The following were children of the second wife: George, married to Margaret Haney; Henry; Michael; William, — had been a soldier in the late war; Noah; Catharine, married to John Walters; Sarah, married to Mr. .... Glouch.

2. CATHARINE, married to John Witters.

3. JOHN, married to Magdalena Meyer, a daughter of the Schaefferstown Christopher Meyer, and consequently, a granddaughter of John Henry Meyer. (See pages 30–32.) He lives on the western part of the old Mühlbach tract. I visited him in the Fall of 1883 and received considerable information for these pages from the family. He was born in 1808 or 1809, and is still living, Nov. 1889. His wife is dead. *Children:* — John H., born 1835, married to Amanda Robinson, lives also on the old Mühlbach tract. William H. H., married to Lizzie Robinson, sister of John's wife; Amanda; Agnes, married Charles Garman; Monroe, married to Frances Stover; Tillie, married to John Stover.

4. Michael, was born Nov. 19, 1810; is married to Lucy Ann Krall. The family lives about one and a half miles south-west of the Mühlbach homestead. Michael is a pleasant and intelligent gentleman, and is quite well posted on Meyer history. He is of short stature, as most of his great-grandfather John's descendants are. He says, we call the Campbellstown Meyers (Christopher's sons) the "big Meyers". He remembers how, when he was a boy, the Pennsvalley (Centre County) Meyers used to send hounds in boxes to his father. All the Meyers of that period were hunters. I visited the family twice in 1883. *Children:*—Israel, born in 1835, married first to Catharine Betts, second, to Caroline Friese, lives in Ohio; Levi, married Eda Heckman, lives in Ohio;

Catharine, married to Wm. Miller, she died in 1880; Solomon, married Catharine Banter, lives at Schaefferstown, Pa.; Caroline, married Frank Goss; John, married to Amanda Royer.

5. Elizabeth, married to J. B. Smith of Berks County, Pa., who represented his county three successive terms in the Legislature.

ISSUE WITH SECOND WIFE—CHRISTINA LISE:

6. Henry, married to Sarah Miller. He was born Jan. 28, 1815; died Nov. 1, 1881. His wife was born Jan. 1, 1819. Henry owned the old homestead and his widow and two sons reside there now (1883). I visited there several times during the Summer of 1883, and received many facts for this sketch from the widow and from papers which she kindly permitted me to examine. It was she who gave me the information about the original buildings near the spring. Her husband's grandmother, Catharine (Schaeffer) Meyer, used to say that the buildings had been put up by the "old

folks", that is, by the Meyers who came from Germany. (See page 18.) Charles M. Zerba, Esq., of Lebanon, Pa., writes me, June 25, 1888, that the farm which had been in possession of the Meyers so many generations, has at last passed into other hands, J. Monroe Zimmerman now owning it. See note, page 15. But this does not include the whole of the original tract, only the eastern part or half. *Children:* — Sarah, married to Uriah Kryder; Henry, married Clarissa Dissinger, great-granddaughter of the Schaefferstown Christopher Meyer. Henry was born March 3, 1850, died Feb. 26, 1886. He and his brother Thomas lived on the old farm at the spring and were the last Meyer owners of it;

Ida Christina, married to John Achey, lives at Lebanon, Pa.; Thomas, married Celicia Strickler.

7. Mary, married Henry Fisher. Indiana.

8. Sarah, married Cyrus Kryder.

9. Leah, married to George Dager.

II. Michael (John, John, Gr. Meyer), died single prior to 1795. He at one time owned the old homestead at Mühlbach.

III. George (John, John, Gr. Meyer), died single, aged about twenty-two.

IV. Henry (John, John, Gr. Meyer), was married to Lizzie Strock. He lived at Gravel Hill, Lebanon Co., Pa.

ISSUE:—

1. John, married to Anna Behm. He died in 1855, aged 54 years. *Children:* — John, married to Catharine Keim.

He is deceased ; Henry (dec'd), married to Lovina Miller ; Michael B., born March 20, 1845, died at Harrisburg, Pa., July 13, 1889. Disease, congestive fever. Lies buried at Derry, Dauphin Co. He was married to Fannie Strickler. She was born Jan. 13, 1847. Michael lived formerly at Derry, Dauphin Co., where he owned a fine farm. He was a man of intelligence, and influential in his locality, having filled at different periods nearly all the elective offices of his township. In 1877 he resigned the office of school-director to become County Commissioner of Dauphin County, which position he filled two terms. At the time of his death he was Prison Warden at Harrisburg, which office he had held over two years. Michael had been raised by his uncle, Mr. Behm, ex-commissioner of Dauphin County ; he was a poor boy, but by a close application to his books, he acquired a good education in the schools of his neighborhood, and by industry and perseverance amassed considerable property. During Lee's invasion of Pennsylvania Michael shouldered the musket in defense of our State against the Confederates. In politics he was a thorough Republican, and in a political contest was seldom vanquished. He was a man of large stature, noble bearing, benevolent disposition, greatly beloved by his family and highly esteemed by his numerous friends. I visited the family at Derry in the Fall of 1883 and again in 1889 at Harrisburg. Widow Meyer is at present filling the office of Prison Warden left vacant by the death of her husband. The couple were married Nov. 6, 1866, and had nine children. *Children :* — Annie M.; Frances F.; Harvey S.; Ada S.; Lizzie G.; Clara S.; John S.; Emma S.; Mary V.

2. MICHAEL, married to Elizabeth Horner, both are dead.

3. MARY, married to Jacob Hemperly.

4. SARAH, married to Andrew Loy.

5. SUSAN, married to Jacob Goss.

6. ELENOR, was married to Henry Meyer, son of "big" Michael near Rebersburg, Pa. She was born Feb. 12, 1809, died Sept. 28, 1884.

7. ELIZABETH, married Ulrich Weltmer.

V. BARBARA (John, John, Gr. Meyer), was married to John Loudermilk.

VI. CATHARINE (John, John, Gr. Meyer), was not married.

VII. ELIZABETH (John, John, Gr. Meyer).

II. HENRY or JOHN HENRY (John, Gr. Meyer), married to Anna Engle, so stated on an old deed (see page 22), but his granddaughter, Mrs. Martha Zerbe, says his wife was a Miss Ruth. The date of his birth was not ascertained; it is said he died Nov., 1812. George Meyer, Dauphin, Pa., states he often heard his grandmother, Catharine (Schaeffer) Meyer, say that Henry was the only brother that his grandfather John had; and that at one time he owned the Mühlbach homestead, but being unable to keep it, his grandfather John (Henry's brother) bought it at the solicitation of his grandmother Catharine, so that the old home should remain in the Meyer name. See deed, page 22.

There were three children, two sons and one daughter.

I. JOHN GEORGE (Henry, John, Gr. Meyer) was married to a Miss Harnish.

ISSUE:—

1. JOHN, was married to a Miss Seibert. He died about the year 1843, aged about sixty years.

2. JACOB, dec'd, was married to Elizabeth Shall.

3. MICHAEL, married to Mary Erb. Live out West somewhere.

4. HENRY, married to a Miss Erb, sister of Michael's wife.

5. ANNA MARIA, married Andrew Capp.

6. MARY, married John Parson.

7. CATHARINE, married to Jonas Moore.

II. CATHARINE (Henry, John, Gr. Meyer), was married to Jacob (?) Miller.

III. CHRISTOPHER (Henry, John, Gr. Meyer), was married twice, first to a Miss Eckert, second to widow Hoffman, whose maiden name was Catharine Krum. This lady was an inmate of the house in which occurred the Sheetz murder in 1797; she was then a little girl and was present when the murder was committed. The place is not far from Mühlbach. Christopher was born Sept. 5, 1761; died Jan. 5, 1822. He lived at Schaefferstown, Lebanon Co., Pa., and must not be confounded with the Christopher Meyer who lived at Campbellstown, same county. The list of children was given by John Meyer, Mühlbach, son-in-law, and corrected later by Charles M. Zerbe, Esq., Lebanon, Pa.

ISSUE WITH FIRST WIFE—SEVEN CHILDREN.

1. JOHN married Catharine Wolfersperger. Lives at Breathodsville, Md. *Children:* — John, married a Miss Mussina, near Hagerstown, Md.; Israel, married to Salina Everly, Schaefferstown, Pa.; Sarah, married to John Hill, Sheridan, Pa.; Susanna, married Michael Groh, Schaefferstown, Pa.

2. MICHAEL, married Miss M. Crotzer.

3. SUSAN, married to Jacob Funk, Maryland.

4. ELIZABETH, married to Henry Schaeffer, grandson of Alexander Schaeffer, who laid out Schaefferstown, Pa. See page 25. Clara (Dissinger), wife of Henry Meyer, who lived on the old Mühlbach farm till recently, is a granddaughter of this couple. Elizabeth was born Aug. 24, 1796; died July 3, 1864. *Children:*—Catharine, married Jeremiah Magee; Rebecca, married William Dissinger; Infant: Dr. Samuel M., born 1823; died Dec. 29, 1872.

5. MARGARET, married to Michael Stroch.

6. CATHARINE, married Joe Crotzer, Maryland.

7. MARY, married John Krall.

ISSUE WITH SECOND WIFE, FOUR CHILDREN.

8. SARAH, married John Krall. She died about the year 1863.

9. MAGDALENA, married to John Meyer, who lives on the western part of the Mühlbach tract. See page 26. She was born in 1814; died Nov. 6, 1879.

10. Martha, married to Dr. Jonathan Zerbe, Schaefferstown, Pa. She is still living (1888). She contributed considerable information for these pages, forwarded through the kindness of her son, Charles M. *Children:* — Charles M., married to Rebecca Yearsley, Phila. The family live at Lebanon, Pa., where Mr. Zerbe is practising law; Agnes E. (deceased), was married to Dr. George Mays; Dr. Thomas T., married to Emma E. Taylor; Jennie M., married to J. F. Hickernell; Dr. B. Frank, married to Ida S. Lauser. Last three children live at Schaefferstown, Pa.

11. Lydia, married Ed. Becker.

III. Anna Margaret (John, Gr. Meyer), was married to Jacob Neff.

IV. Elizabeth (John, Gr. Meyer), was married to John Moore.

V. Barbara (John, Gr. Meyer), was married to Ludwig Miller.

JACOB MEYER[1] (son of the Meyer from Germany) was the second son, and was born at Mühlbach. The date of his birth was not ascertained, nor the date of his decease definitely. There is no tombstone with an inscription, and if there are any positive records anywhere on the subject, I failed to discover them. Letters of administration were granted Samuel and John Haas to settle up his estate, dated Feb. 24, 1808, and it is probable he died only a short time previous to that date. Tradition and some papers in my possession point to about the same period. He was about seventy-five years old, states Maj. John Meyer, a grandson.

Jacob lived at Mühlbach until about the year 1768, when he moved with his family to Penn's township, now part of Snyder County, Pa., and purchased a large tract of land lying west about three-fourths of a mile from the present site of Freeburg, formerly named Straubsburg, after its founder, Peter Straub, and was one of the early settlers in that section. Andrew Moor, a Mr. Glass and Mr. Straub had preceded him. The family suffered the usual hardships incident to frontier life. Their flour was brought from Mühlbach on horseback. Yet there must have been grist-mills more convenient at that date. On one of those trips for supplies Jacob's brother, Christopher, came along to the new country, and while crossing Peter's mountain, north of Harrisburg, the pack saddle-straps gave way, and the packs rolled down the mountain. Then Christopher got out of humor, and berated Jacob for moving into the distant wilderness whence

---

1. *Note.*—Or John Jacob. Hon. Jacob G. Meyer states that each of the son's first name was *John*. But they are not found written thus in old manuscripts. However, it was not an unusual custom at that period to name a whole family of sons *John*, employing a middle name Henry, George, Jacob or whatever it might be to distinguish them.

no roads would ever be made; to which the latter replied that sometime in the future excellent roads would be constructed. And of course Jacob's prophecy came true, for around the end of that same mountain which they crossed along a narrow path there are now a fine carriage road, a canal and a double track for cars, while just across the river there is another railroad track. Probably it was, to resume our narrative, on this trip that a bag was torn open by a brush along the path and the flour spilled on the ground.

Sometime during the Revolutionary War Jacob moved back again with his family to Mühlbach, probably to be more secure from the annoying depredations of hostile Indians. He was drafted and served in the army, but in what capacity or for what length of time was not ascertained. His oldest son, Philip, as will be stated more fully elsewhere, was also in the army. His son Henry[1] (grandfather) was at the age of sixteen connected with an organization of "home-guards" or scouts to protect the settlement against the Indians, and served at intervals. It appears the family returned from Mühlbach to their home in Penn's township (Freeburg) before the close of the war. Indians sometimes lurked about their home, but never molested them, being afraid, perhaps, of the pack of fierce dogs kept on the place. On one occasion several Indians were observed across the clearing, some distance from the house; the boys and dogs gave chase, but did not overtake them. Several Indian families lived within a short distance of the Meyer home, and his—Mr. Meyer's—children used to play with the Indian children. During the

---

1. *Note.*—Grandfather (Henry), like many others of that period, had made a vow to kill every Indian he would meet. So after all hostilities had subsided, he happened to meet one of his old foes in a tavern somewhere, but the forelorn and piteous aspect of the poor Indian excited grandfather's sympathy rather than his animosity, and, instead of scalping him, he gave him a huge piece of tobacco!

Indian troubles the male members of these Indian families would generally be away from home, and it was suspected they were out on scalping expeditions, though they were on friendly terms with their near white neighbors.

Jacob kept a sort of a tavern at Straubsburg (Freeburg), and Col. Samuel Miles used to stop with him on his journeys from his home in Philadelphia to his lands in Penns, Brush and Nittany valleys (now Centre Co.) and back, and it was through the intimate acquaintance thus formed with Col. Miles that grandfather Henry came to purchase a tract of land from him in Brushvalley. It is said Jacob protested against his son's purchasing any land in Brushvalley, for the reason that there would never any roads be opened into it! Jacob and his sons used to hunt in the valley long before any settlers moved into it, and he did not suppose it would ever be any good for anything else! Yet he lived to see his mistake; for in his old age he paid a visit to his sons in the valley, about the year 1803–1806, and beheld the wilderness converted into fertile fields, and the desert made to blossom as the rose.

In 1800 Christopher Meyer, son of Campbellstown Christopher, came to Freeburg (then Straubsburg), and in 1801 "Big John," another son of the latter, also settled in that vicinity. (These dates are given by Fred. C. Meyer, Freeburg.) Therefore, in 1801, there were in that place Jacob and several of his sons, and their cousins Christopher and "Big John." Grandfather Henry had then moved to Brushvalley already, and I am not quite certain whether his brother John Jacob had not moved away, also then, to Pine Creek, Lycoming County, Pa. At present there are many descendants about Freeburg of Christopher and John, but not one male descendant of great-grandfather Jacob.

Jacob was married to Miss Susan Zartman, born in Germany, so say uncle John and Reuben Meyer, grandsons. But in an old power of attorney in my possession, given by Jacob Meyer, Sr., to his son Michael, dated 1801, mention is made of Jacob's wife as being *Susanna Ream*, daughter of Peter Ream, Dauphin County, Pa. The instrument was given to secure the wife's legacy, and seems to be positive evidence as to her maiden name. The paper alludes to her as being then deceased. In a sketch of Michael Meyer in a history of Summit County, Ohio, her maiden name is also given as Susan Ream. One of the Greningers of Sugar Valley, Clinton County, Pa., an early settler there, was married to her sister. Great-grandmother Meyer (Jacob's wife) was not a large woman, but what she lacked in stature was fully compensated for in grit and temper. She used to whip her boys after they were full grown! Some of them were almost giants, and no doubt they could stand up and meekly take a whipping without suffering much pain. The boys, of whom there were six, viz.:—Philip, John Jacob, John George, Henry, Michael and Christopher, were not allowed to grow up in idleness, but were early put to work. One of their occupations was weaving,—probably during bad weather, when out-door work could not be done, and as they were rather fond of constructing things with carpenters' tools, they sometimes neglected their work at the loom; then if their mother would discover the objects on which they were exercising their ingenuity and wasting their time, she would smash them, and pitch the fragments into the fire. The boys were careful not needlessly to expose their handicraft. Father used to say the boys were of a rather hilarious disposition, and attended all the parties and balls within reasonable distance; they made their own violins, which some could play with considerable skill, and as their mother was opposed to gatherings of the kind, she would demolish their musical instruments without ceremony whenever misfortune would reveal to her their hiding place. It is said that on a certain occasion she dressed in disguise, went to one of the parties where the boys were in attendance, and gave them a whipping then and there. On one occasion when her son Philip had tackled a big Irishman, and got the worst of it, she remarked to him, as she beheld the rainbow tints on his face, "Well, did you get a licking again?" Philip admitted it was so, but said he was going to learn the pugilistic art, if it cost his head. And he did become proficient! Yet she was a good mother, and labored hard and faithfully to raise her numerous family amid the hardships of frontier life, and her big sons dearly loved her, and would have sacrificed their lives in her defense.

Jacob was not a large man, was of a kindly disposition and not inclined to be quarrelsome, but it is said he seemed rather pleased when he heard that his sons came off victorious in their many pugilistic contests. Both he and his wife are buried in the old cemetery at Freeburg; neither has a tombstone with an inscription. Their son John George is buried in the same cemetery; as also another son, Christopher, probably. I visited the cemetery in 1883, and father had visited it a number of years before, but neither was able to locate any of the graves.

List of Children:

Catharine. *See* page 39.

Barbara. *See* page 40.

Philip. *See* page 41.

John Jacob. *See* page 51.

John George. *See* page 58.

Henry. *See* page 61.

Michael. *See* page 82.

Christopher. *See* page 87.

I. CATHARINE (daughter of Jacob, son of Gr. Meyer) was the oldest of the family, but the dates of birth or death were not discovered. She was married to John Meyer, and the couple moved on a tract of land in Brushvalley (Centre County, Pa.), which was purchased subsequently by grandfather Henry Meyer — brother-in-law of John. The latter was one of the first settlers in the Valley, and may have located in it as early as the year 1792. He cleared considerable land, and put up the first buildings on the tract near Elk Creek, and no doubt planted the apple trees there, some of which still (1889) remain — one measuring eleven and a half feet in circumference. John Meyer had erected an oil mill at Oil Gap, some distance east of Woodward, Pa., before he came to Brushvalley, and grandfather Henry Meyer had done the mill-wright work on it. From an old receipt in my possession, I find he sold his interest in his land to grandfather Henry Meyer, May 2, 1797, and moved to Kentucky, where he erected a distillery. Very little was heard about the family afterwards. His brother Philip, his son-in-law Jacob Kreiger and Tobias Pickle moved to Kentucky at the same time, thence some, if not all, to Ohio. Father used to say that this John Meyer was a cousin of his father; but others denied it. I could not find the link of the relationship. He was a red-headed, raw-boned man, large stature; and had been a soldier in the Revolutionary War. He was in the Battle of Brandywine, and was a brave soldier, but when the retreat began he soon outstripped all the rest running.

I have not a list of John's children, except a partial one furnished me by John P. Meyer, of Felicity, O. He states that a Meyer family, who were *cousins* of his father (Philip) coming from the same place (Brushvalley), located near where his father settled. He names three brothers, viz.:— John, George and Jacob; and thinks there were three or

6

four sisters, and mentions Susan and Mary. No doubt these were John's children. Philip could not have had any other cousins in that section. See page 43.

II. Barbara (daughter of Jacob, son of Gr. Meyer) was married to Michael Motz. The family lived at the east end of Pennsvalley, Centre County, Pa. Samuel Motz, a grandson, owns part of the farm now (1889). Barbara took care of her brother Henry (grandfather) while he had a malignant fever, of which his wife had died a short time before, and by careful attendance brought him through. See page 62. She and her husband are buried at St. Paul, near their home. I found the following record on a stone which marks the grave of Michael Motz: —"1830 ...... Michael Motz, Alt, 85 years. ...... 23 tag." I could not decipher all of the inscription. Barbara, no doubt, lies by his side. From the Motz's old family Bible now in possession of Samuel Motz, who lives on the old homestead, I copy a list of Barbara's children. There were seven daughters and one son :—

I. Eva, born, 1772; married John Wise, Pennsvalley.

II. Susanna, born, 1774 ; married George Wise.

III. Barbara, born, 1775 ; married Martin Wise.

IV. Catharine, born, Nov. 11, 1781 ; died, Feb. 12, 1836 ; was married to John Harper.

V. Elizabeth, born, 1783 ; married to Jacob Hess.

VI. Margaret, born, 1785 ; married Conrad Wise.

VII. Henry, born, Feb. 15, 1788 ; died, Jan. 31, 1847. He was married to his cousin Barbara Meyer, daughter of John

Jacob Meyer, Jersey Shore, Pa. See page 54. She was born Aug. 8, 1796; died, Oct. 22, 1842. Both are buried at St. Paul, near Woodward, Pa.

ISSUE:

1. SAMUEL, married Lydia Hess,—lives on the old homestead, Pennsvalley, near Woodward, Pa.

2. ELIAS, married a Miss Showalter,—Woodward, Pa.

3. REBECCA, married Andrew Auble.

4. ELIZA, married Jacob Wise.

5. MATILDA, married Daniel Smith.

VIII. SOPHIA, born 1794; married to Abraham High.

III. PHILIP (son of Jacob, son of Gr. Meyer) was married to Margaret Morr, sister of his brother John Jacob's wife Julia, daughters of Andrew Morr,[1] one of the early settlers in the region where Freeburg, Pa., is now located. The respective family histories of the Meyers and Morrs have been

---

1. *Note.*—Andrew Morr came from Germany, and settled near the present site of Freeburg, Pa., sometime prior to 1770. He took up a large tract of land and improved it. There was erected on his farm a stockade for protection against the Indians. He and Jacob Meyer were near neighbors, and both pioneers in the new country. Morr was a prominent member of the Lutheran Church; and a man of influence in his neighborhood. He died in 1805, and is buried at Freeburg, Pa. There were seven children. I copy a partial list from a sketch prepared by Miss Mary E. Morr, West Salem, O., for a Reunion of the Morr family, June 9, 1887. Of the seven children, Miss Morr names only four, viz:—

I. GEORGE, oldest child; died in 1818; buried at Aaronsburg, Pa. Married to Catharine Diefenbach. Had been a soldier in the Revolu-

running in parallel streams for over a century with frequent intermingling of their branches all along their course. The first record of marriage between the two families is that of Philip Meyer and Margaret Morr, which occurred about the year 1780 ; and the members of the families still continue to intermarry in Ohio. Philip was the oldest of the sons ; heavy built, muscular and active, but not as tall as his brothers. He was a noted wrestler in his day, and was not averse to contests of a more serious nature, as his numerous experiments in that line seem to demonstrate. But that was in an age when physical power was at a premium. The man who could leap the greatest distance, could kick the highest and hit the hardest blows was a hero and received the applause of society. There was a vast amount of hard work to do in those pioneer days, and for want of labor-saving machinery, it had to be accomplished by sheer physical force. Hence, any exercise which tended to muscular development, or exhibited physical vigor in its greatest perfection, was cherished and applauded.—Philip served in the Revolutionary War, being a member of Capt. Ben. Weiser's company. Adam Schaeffer was Lieutenant of the company, and subsequently became captain by promotion. On his return from the army Philip settled down to domestic life near Freeburg for a number of years, thence moved to Brushvalley, Centre Co.,

---

tionary War. Moved to Centre County, Pa., in 1792. Had twelve children:—George, Philip, Peter, Mary, Andrew, Elizabeth, John, Adam, Michael, Daniel, Benjamin, Samuel. All but Adam moved to Ohio.

II. Philip, lived at Freeburg; died in 1826. John Jacob was one of his sons.

III. Margaret, born August 20, 1759; died March 12, 1829. Married Philip Meyer.

IV. Julian, born July 18, 1770; died Nov. 8, 1824. Married John Jacob Meyer.

Pa., and bought a tract of land about a mile east of the present post village of Wolf's Store. This was about the year 1802. His brother Henry had then been in the valley five years, while Michael, another brother, came three years later. Mr. Meyer, the subject of our sketch, was of a liberal disposition,—was kind to his family, generous to his neighbors, and a useful citizen in his township. For many years he was supervisor of Miles township, serving in that capacity in 1815, when the public road from Wolf's Store across the mountains to Pennsvalley was made. Philip was a consistent member of the Reformed Church, and mother states he experienced religion in his declining days and died a happy Christian. A short time before his death, he remarked to Mr. Fred. C. Meyer, of Freeburg, who visited him, "I am ready to die." He breathed his last April 27, 1831, aged 75 years, 5 months and 13 days. His wife was born Aug. 20, 1759; died March 12, 1829. Both are buried in the Lutheran and Reformed cemetery, Rebersburg, Pa. One tombstone marks the graves of both. Their descendants are legion and are all out West, mostly in Ohio and Iowa.

There were eleven children, seven sons and four daughters.

I. PHILIP (Philip, Jacob, Gr. Meyer) was born about the year 1780, died Dec. 19, 1858. Moved to Kentucky about the year 1801, and married his first wife, Elizabeth Meyer,[1] about

---

1. *Note.*—John P. Meyer, Felicity, O., states in a letter, dated March 14, 1884, that his mother's maiden name was Elizabeth Meyer, and he thinks her father's name was Philip; he was not related to his father. The family had come from the same place as his father, and consisted of four sons, viz.:—Jacob, John, Abraham and George; and five daughters, viz.:—Elizabeth, Mary, Catharine, Susan and Margaret. No doubt this is the Philip Meyer who had leased and partly improved a tract in Brushvalley, Centre Co., Pa., which John P.'s grandfather, Philip Meyer, subsequently purchased. See page 42. If so, he was a brother of John Meyer, husband of Catharine Meyer. See page 39.

the same date. With his first wife he had eight children. She died about the year 1814. The name of the second wife was not stated by John P. Meyer, who furnished these facts. With the second wife Philip had also eight children.

ISSUE—FIRST WIFE:

1. HENRY, born about the year 1802; was drowned when aged about fifteen years.

2. ANDREW—died in infancy.

3. SUSAN, married to James Cook.

4. MARGARET, married Samuel Gibson.

5. SAMUEL, married to Mary Meyer, daughter of Jacob Meyer, a brother of Philip's wife Elizabeth. The couple were therefore first cousins.

6. SARAH, married William Metier, who was from Penna.

7. JOHN P., born April 23, 1809; married to Mahala Miller, April 5, 1843. John P. furnished these facts in reference to his father's family. His address was then Felicity, Ohio.

8. ELIZABETH, married William Metzger.

ISSUE WITH SECOND WIFE:

9. JOSEPH; 10. LEVI; 11. MICHAEL; 12. GEORGE; 13. ISAAC; 14. MARY ANN; 15. MATILDA; 16. CATHARINE.

II. GEORGE (Philip, Jacob, Gr. Meyer) married Rosena Kreamer. He moved to Marion County, Ohio, in August, 1832. Died about the year 1842.

ISSUE:

1. CATHARINE; 2. PHILIP; 3. GEORGE; 4. MARY; 5. SAMUEL; 6. ROSENA.

III. JACOB (Philip, Jacob, Gr. Meyer) married to Mary Stein. The family lived for sometime near Hamburg, Clinton County, Pa., thence moved to Wayne County, O., but now Ashland County, as the latter was taken from Wayne and Richland.

ISSUE:

1. JONATHAN, married to Elizabeth Spangler. Live at Ashland, O.

2. GEORGE, married Elizabeth Morr, descendant of Andrew Morr. See note, page 41. Family resides at Ashland, O. George was born Nov. 12, 1822; his wife is about four years younger. Nine children. The parents and their daughter Effie visited Rebersburg, Pa., Nov., 1882, and from them was received a list of Jacob's (George's father's) family.

3. JACOB married Elizabeth Horn, Kansas.

4. MARGARET married to Samuel Meng. She lives at Ashland, O. Widow (1882).

5. ELIZA married to Emanuel Morr. Widow (1882), lives at Ashland, O.

6. MARY married to Joseph Echlebarger. She is dead. Lived at Ashland, O.

7. CATHARINE, deceased, was married to John Echlebarger, lived at Ashland, O.

8. BENJAMIN, married to Mattie Cowan. His wife deceased. Benjamin is a physician, had been a member of the Ohio Legislature.

9. DANIEL, married to Elizabeth Felger, Ashland, O.

IV. HENRY (Philip, Jacob, Gr. Meyer) was married to Barbara Foreman, whose father used to live near Philip Meyer's home, Brushvalley, Centre Co., Pa. Henry moved to Ohio. His wife, Barbara, died (or was buried), April 24, 1885, aged 90 years, 20 days.

ISSUE:

1. GEORGE, married Annie Herr. He was born about the year 1815. The family lived in Wayne County, O.

2. JOHN, married to Annie Morr, Wayne Co., O.

3. MARGARET, married Samuel Herr, Ashland, O.

4. DANIEL, deceased, was married to Sarah Kanaga. Lived in Wayne Co., O.

5. SUSAN, married to David Herr. Lived in Wayne Co., O. She is a widow.

6. HENRY, deceased.

7. ELIZA, married Jacob Ball, Ashland, O.

8. WILLIAM, married to Mary Miller, Ashland, O.

9. REUBEN, single (1882).

V. JOHN (Philip, Jacob, Gr. Meyer) married Sept. 21, 1821, to Mary M. Gast, daughter of Christian Gast,[1] who at one time lived on the farm now owned by Samuel Gramly, Brush-

---

1. *Note.*—John Nicholas Gast and John Christian Gast were brothers, and came from Würtemberg, landing at Philadelphia about Oct. 7, 1755. *See Rupp's Collection of 30,000 Emigrant names. Page 349.* Nicholas settled at Harrisburg (now) while Christian settled at same period on Middle Creek, now Snyder County, Pa., thence moved to Brushvalley, Centre Co., Pa. Christian was born

valley, Centre Co., Pa. The family moved from Pennsylvania to Marion County, O., in 1833, thence to Scott County, Iowa, May 9, 1851, where they purchased a large tract of land. I remember seeing John, who paid a visit to Pennsylvania sometime before the late War. He was not very tall, but heavy set. He was born Oct. 15, 1794; died Jan. 23, 1872. His wife was born March 21, 1803; died Oct. 19, 1853. I am indebted to Mr. J. L. Gast, son-in-law of Mr. Meyer for list of children (1884). Beside the children here named two had died in infancy. I believe all of John's decendants live in Iowa. Two of John's sisters, Elizabeth and Margaret were married to Gasts—brothers of his wife.

April 23, 1726; died about the year 1805. His wife, Christina Brandt, also came from Würtemberg; she was born Oct. 29, 1729, and died about the year 1803; both are buried at Rebersburg, Pa. Christian had three children:—I. John Nicholas, born April 21, 1760; died Dec. 2, 1810; his wife, Anna Catharine Kibe, was born Nov. 15, 1771; died Oct. 11, 1863; both buried at Rebersburg, Pa. The family had moved into Brushvalley about the year 1794. *Children*:—1. John Adam; 2. George; 3. Henry, lives at Mifflinburg, Pa.; 4. John, lives at Mifflinburg, Pa.; 5. Barbara, m. Geo. Tate; 6. Catharine, m. Dan'l Conser, both dead, buried at Rebersburg, Pa.; 7. Christina, m. Hon. John Reynolds, widow, now (1889) in her 90th year, lives at Rebersburg, Pa.; 8. Mary, m. Jacob Wolf, deceased; she lives near Rebersburg, Pa. 9. Susan, m. Paul Wolf, widow; 10. Elizabeth, m. Solomon Crotzer.

II. Christian, married Margaret Borer. Moved to Brushvalley in 1793; thence about the year 1808, to Blair County, Pa. Had been a soldier in the Revolutionary War. *Children*:— 1. Christian, m. Elizabeth Meyer, daughter of Philip Meyer. See page 50. Lived at Middletown, O. 2. John, m. Margaret Meyer, sister of Christian's wife Elizabeth, Ohio. 3. George, m. Susan Lamer; 4. Jacob; 5. William; 6. Samuel; 7. Catharine, m. Wm. Lamer; 8. Mary M., m. John Meyer, brother of Elizabeth and Margaret just named, Iowa, see above. 9. Margaret; 10. Sallie.

III. Catharine, married Mr. Maurer; moved West.

ISSUE:

1. PHILIP, married Mariah Fegley in 1847. He was born May 26, 1822. Four children.

2. CHRISTIAN, born July 21, 1823; married Harriet McElvaine in 1846. Five children.

3. MARGARET, born Feb. 22, 1825; married to J. L. Gast in 1845. Husband born Feb. 3, 1823. Three children (Mr. Gast furnished list of John Meyer's children, 1884). Princeton, Iowa.

4. WILLIAM, born Nov. 13, 1826; married in 1854 to Ellen Harte. Four children.

5. SARAH, born June 15, 1829; married in 1851 to H. L. Gast. Nine children.

6. CATHARINE, born Feb. 22, 1831; married in 1854 to Joe Coe. Four children.

7. DANIEL, born April 7, 1833; married in 1854 to Rose Spayd. Five children.

8. JOHN, born May 5, 1835; died March, 1883. Married Nancy Carter. Wife deceased. One child.

9. ELIAS, born April 23, 1840; married in 1862 to Susan Graham. Two children.

10. LEBUS, born Feb. 19, 1842; married Feb. 6, 1866 to Lizzie Schnellbacher.

VI. BENJAMIN, (Philip, Jacob, Gr. Meyer) married to Margaret, daughter of John Wolfart, who lived near neighbor to Benjamin's father in Brushvalley, Centre Co., Pa. The family moved to Ohio.

ISSUE:

1. CATHARINE, married first to Andrew Morr; second to Jacob Poorman, son of Melchior Poorman, Brushvalley, Centre County, Pa. Lived in Ohio.

2. MARGARET, married Samuel Morr, Ashland, O.

VII. SAMUEL (Philip, Jacob, Gr. Meyer) was born Dec. 26, 1805; died Sept. 19, 1884. He was first married, in 1828, to Esther Reynolds, sister of Hon. John Reynolds, Rebersburg, Pa. His first wife died in 1833. July 7, 1836, Samuel was married to his second wife, Susan J. Russell; she died July 22, 1874. The family moved first to Ohio, thence to Iowa, near Garvin. I am under obligations to their daughter Lyde, for these facts.

ISSUE WITH FIRST WIFE.

1. JOHN F.

2. SAMUEL, born Nov. 30, 1830; married Rebecca McElvaine, Tama County, Iowa.

3. MARGARET, born Nov. 24, 1832; married to Philip Morr, Wayne County, Ohio.

ISSUE WITH SECOND WIFE.

4. SARAH, born June 13, 1837; married William Gast.

5. ELIZABETH MARY, born Nov. 29, 1838; died Feb. 22, 1856

6. ESTHER JANE, born Dec. 22, 1840; married Joseph A. Russell.

7. SUSANNA E., born March 8, 1843; married Francis H Allen.

8. ADELIA P., born Sept. 13, 1845; died Oct. 20, 1864.

9. NANCY ELIZABETH, born March 11, 1848.

10. ROXANA P., born Sept. 21, 1850; married Charles Reush.

11. ORA EVA, born Feb. 23, 1856; died Feb. 20, 1864.

12. FLORENCE MAY, born Jan. 14, 1861; married Ed. M. Strohm.

VIII. BARBARA (Philip, Jacob, Gr. Meyer) married to John Motz.

IX. ELIZABETH (Philip, Jacob, Gr. Meyer), born May 17, 1792; died Dec. 17, 1865: She was married June 8, 1813 to Christian Gast, son of Christian Gast. See note, page 46. Her husband died Dec. 29, 1858, aged 68 years, 4 months and 20 days. The family moved from Pennsylvania to Marion County, O., April 27, 1832. Mr. Gast purchased a large tract on the banks of the Sciota, and laid out a town, which he named Middletown. He was a member of the Lutheran Church, and contributed liberally towards its support.

ISSUE:

1. MARGARET; 2. ELIZABETH; 3. PHILIP; 4. CHRISTIAN; 5. CATHARINE; 6. GEORGE; 7. SARAH; 8. DAVID,[1] born Dec. 17, 1829; married to Kate M. Rowe, Prospect, O.; 9. MARY; 10. ABIGAIL.

---

1. *Note.*—David Gast visited Centre County, Pa., during the Winter of 1882 and 1883. From him was received a list of the family.

X. Margaret (Philip, Jacob, Gr. Meyer) married John Gast, brother of Christian, married to her sister, Elizabeth. And these two were brothers of Mary Magdelena Gast, wife of John Meyer. See page 46. And all three were children of Christian Gast, who lived west of Rebersburg one and a-half miles, an early settler,—thence moved to Frankstown, Blair County, Pa. Margaret and her husband also moved to Prospect, Ohio, in the year 1834. She died May 24, 1878, in her 82nd year. Her husband died in 1872, in his 80th year. Descendants in Ohio and Iowa.

ISSUE:

1. Sarah; 2. Abigail; 3. William; 4. Catharine; 5. Samuel; 6. John; 7. Margaret; 8. Levi; 9. Elizabeth.

XI. Catharine (Philip, Jacob, Gr. Meyer) was married to Daniel Kreamer, a brother of Abraham Kreamer, who was married to Maria Buchtel. See note, page 58. The family lived at Uniontown, O.

IV. John Jacob (son of Jacob, son of Gr. Meyer) was married to Julia Morr, sister of his brother Philip's wife, Margaret. See note, page 41. The family moved from near Freeburg, Pa., to Pine Creek, near Jersey Shore, Pa., where a fine tract of land was purchased. At what date Jacob removed to his new home, I could not determine, but I suppose it was about the year 1800. It is said that in physical appearance he resembled his brother Henry (grandfather); they were greatly attached to each other, and visits between them were frequent. Jacob died in 1813; his illness resulting from drinking too freely at a spring of very cold water on a certain occasion when he had been overheated while out in the woods hunting. He lies buried in the old cemetery at Pine Creek, near Jersey Shore, Pa. No tombstone marks his grave. His son, Samuel, lies buried by his side. His wife, Julia, was born July 18, 1770; died Nov. 8, 1824. The descendants of this couple reside in Clinton and Lycoming counties, Pa., principally.

There were twelve children, five sons and seven daughters.

I. CATHARINE (John Jacob, Jacob, Gr. Meyer) was married to George Meyer, her father's cousin, of Pennsvalley, Pa. She was born Dec. 2, 1788; died March 13, 1858; buried at Aaronsburg, Pa. See page 118.

II. JACOB (John Jacob, Jacob, Gr. Meyer) was married twice, first to Barbara Wise; second, to Martha Clark. His occupation was farming; he lived near Jersey Shore, Pa. His daughter, Mrs. Cummings, says he resembled my father very much; they were fast friends, and visited each other quite often. Jacob was born Dec. 22, 1792; died March 30, 1866; and is buried at Jersey Shore, Pa.

ISSUE—FIRST WIFE:

1. ELIZA, died in infancy.

2. CATHARINE, died in infancy.

3. MARY, deceased, was married to John Nepley.

4. Jacob, married to Rebecca Walise, Ill.

5. MARGARET, deceased, married John Antes, Jersey Shore, Pa.

ISSUE—SECOND WIFE:

6. BARBARA, born April, 19, 1831; married H. A. Cummings. Her husband is dead. She lives at Newberry, Pa.

I visited her Jan. 3, 1888, and received a number of facts for this sketch.

7. MARTHA, married Peter Nepley. She is a widow, and lives at Bloomsburg, Pa.

8. JULIA ANN, married first A. Haganbauch; second, Thomas Holt. She is dead.

9. ELIZABETH, deceased, was married to George Brown.

10. HENRY, married Susan Schenck.

11. MARGERY, deceased, was married to Duncan Campbell.

III. GEORGE (John Jacob, Jacob, Gr. Meyer) was married to Mary Snyder. The family lived near Jersey Shore. George was born Oct. 5, 1794; died Oct. 25, 1849, and is buried in the cemetery midway between the mouth of Pine Creek and Jersey Shore, along the south side of the canal. I presume this is the old burrying-ground in which George's father is interred, and several of his (George's) brothers. George's widow was still living in 1888, aged 83 years, I believe. She resides in Williamsport, Pa.

ISSUE:

1. LUCY ANN, widow, Jersey Shore, Pa., was married to A. Remsdale.

2. BARBARA, died young.

3. ELIZA, died while young.

4. ANDREW, married Margaret Custer, Jersey Shore.

5. HARRIET, married to John N. Gast, son of Adam Gast. See note, page 46. Lives at Lock Haven, Pa. Husband died Dec. 13, 1889.

6. CATHARINE, deceased, was married to P. S. Smith, Jersey Shore.

7. REBECCA, married to Edgar Messimer, Williamsport, Pa.

8. MARY, single, lives with her mother, Williamsport, Pa.

9. MICHAEL, married. Lives at Williamsport, Pa.
10. GEORGE.

11. LYDIA, married to Robert Easton, Williamsport, Pa.

12. ROBERT, died in infancy.

IV. MARY (John Jacob, Jacob, Gr. Meyer) was married to John Fessler. The family lived at or near Newberry, Pa. Mary died April 4, 1857, in the 62nd year of her age. Her husband died Feb. 21, 1859, aged 71 years, 2 months and 12 days; both are buried in the cemetery at Newberry, Pa. I have not a full list of the children, I think; among them are:

1. H. H. FESSLER, born June 20, 1834; married to Wilhelmina Funston. They have one child, Rachel G. Mr. Fessler is an eminent physician, and has a large practice in Newberry (his home) and Williamsport.

2. GEORGE, lives at Newberry, Pa.

3. PHILIP, Attorney-at-Law, lives at Williamsport, Pa.

V. BARBARA (John Jacob, Jacob, Gr. Meyer) was married to her cousin, Henry Motz, son of Michael Motz, who was married to Barbara Meyer (sister of grandfather Henry Meyer). See page 40. The family lived on the old Motz's farm, near Woodward, Pa., East end of Pennsvalley. Barbara was born

Aug. 8, 1796; died Oct. 22, 1842. Her husband was born Feb. 15, 1788; died Jan. 31, 1847; both are buried in the St. Paul church-yard, near Woodward, Pa.

ISSUE:

1. SAMUEL, married Lydia Hess,—live on part of the old homestead, near Woodward.

2. ELIAS, married to a Miss Showalter, — live at Woodward, Pa.

3. ELIZA, married Jacob Wise.

4. REBECCA, married to Andrew Auble.

5. MATILDA, married Daniel Smith.

VI. LYDIA (John Jacob, Jacob, Gr. Meyer), married, first, Thos. Weaver; second, Michael Zeigler. Lived east of Aaronsburg, Pa. She died July 14, 1873, aged 63 years, 3 months and 13 days.

ISSUE:

LOUISA, m. Elias Zellers. Several children died young.

VII. PHILIP (John Jacob, Jacob, Gr. Meyer) was married to Abbie Snyder. The family lived at Pine Creek, near Jersey Shore, Pa. Philip was born Aug. 22, 1805; died Aug. 12, 1867. His wife was born July 9, 1808

ISSUE:

1. ELIZABETH, born March 4, 1828; married to George Keagle; live at Loyalsockville, Pa.

2. JACOB, born Nov. 18, 1829; married Margaret Venemam.

3. GEORGE W., born Feb. 22, 1832; married Elizabeth Wehr, Iowa.

4. JOSEPH S., born Feb. 14, 1834; married Margaret A. Bennet. Live at Pine Creek, near Jersey Shore.

5. HENRY C., born May 17, 1838; married Fanny Dunlap. Pine Creek.

6. ANDREW S., born Dec. 21, 1839; married Hettie A. Kissel. Live at Newberry, Pa. I visited Andrew Jan. 3, 1888, and received from him this list of his father's family.

7. JOHN, born Oct. 17, 1841; died Nov. 22, 1847.

8. PHILIP, born Sept. 17, 1843; married first, Rebecca Oakes; second, Eliza Goulden.

9. BARBARA, born Sept. 24, 1845; died Aug. 30, 1849.

10. JULIET, born Oct. 21, 1847; married John Bennet, Widow, lives at Pine Creek.

11. HARRIET, born Feb. 27, 1851; died Sept. 2, 1852.

VIII. ELIZABETH (John Jacob, Jacob, Gr. Meyer) was married to Thomas Harper. The family lived at the east end of Pennsvalley, Pa. Elizabeth died Aug. 21, 1879, aged 71 years and 8 months. Buried at St. Paul, near Woodward.

ISSUE:

1. MARY A., married to Geo. W. Hutchinson.

2. HENRIETTA, married to Emanuel Motz.

3. EMALINE, married Alex. Motz.

4. KATE, died single.

5. EMELIA, single (1889).

IX. SAMUEL (John Jacob, Jacob, Gr. Meyer), married to Kate Nepley; lived near Jersey Shore, Pa. Both are dead.

ISSUE:

1. CATHARINE, deceased, was married to Wm. Livergood, Jersey Shore.

2. WILLIAM, dead.

3. JANE, deceased, was married to James Fry, Ill.

4. HARRIET, deceased, was married to Ed. Blackwell, Jersey Shore.

5. GEORGE, married............

6. EMELIA, deceased, was married to Wm. Chatman.

X. JOHN (John Jacob, Jacob, Gr. Meyer) was not married. I do not know where John, Samuel and Christina come in as to the order of their ages.

XI. CHRISTINA (John Jacob, Jacob, Gr. Meyer) was married to John Ginder,—lived in Likens Valley, Pa.

XII. JULIA (John Jacob, Jacob, Gr. Meyer) was married to Benjamin F. Lamb. Removed to Illinois. Both are dead. Julia was the youngest of her father's family. I do not know whether this list of her children is complete.

ISSUE:

1. CATHARINE, married to a Mr. Wheeler.

2. JENNIE.

3. ELMINA, died single.

4. CLARA, died single.

5. JOHN F., lives at Wellsville, Kansas.

6. BENJAMIN.

V. JOHN GEORGE (son of Jacob, son of Gr. Meyer) came in possession of his father's farm—the old homestead, near Freeburg, Pa., which he continued to cultivate until his death. The date of his birth I have not been able to ascertain, but it is said he was next to and older than his brother Henry, and is placed in that order on the list. He died about the year 1810, says Fred. C. Meyer, of Freeburg, Pa. His disease was consumption, caused by a cherry-seed, which accidentally lodged in his lungs. He died about a year after the occurance of the accident. George was first married to Elizabeth Buchtel, daughter of John Buchtel.[1] She was a sister of George's brother Michael's wife Agnes, and, also, a sister of Nicholas Bierly's wife Lucy. See note, page 65. Elizabeth was born Sept. 4, 1762; died Sept. 4, 1801, and is buried in the old cemetery near Freeburg. Her grave has a headstone with an inscription, but her husband, who probably

---

1. *Note.*—John Buchtel came from Würtemberg, sailing in the ship Edinburg, Capt. James Russell commanding. He was "qualified" in the court house, Philadelphia, Friday, Sept. 14, 1753, and may have landed about that date. Buchtel, like many other emigrants of that period, was unable to pay for his passage across the ocean, and was therefore bound out to some party, who had bought his services, until the debt was cancelled. While serving in this capacity he became acquainted with a yonng lady in the neighborhood, who also was in servitude for a similar cause,—and they subsequently were married. The family lived for some time at McKee's Half Falls, Snyder County (now), Pa., and thence removed to Brushvalley, Centre County, Pa., about the year 1791-1792. Buchtel died about the year 1809, and is buried at Rebersburg, Pa. His wife accompanied her children out to Ohio about 1812, where she died some time after. All the sons and one or two of the daughters emigrated to Ohio, about Uniontown, Akron, and other points. There were nine children:—

I. JOHN, m. Catharine Snyder. Issue:—Henry, m. Elizabeth, daughter of Michael Meyer. See page 84. 2. John; 3. Herman; 5. Julia.

is buried by her side, has none—at least none with a record. The second wife's maiden name was Mary Brosius. There were ten children, two sons and eight daughters, seven with first wife, and three with second.

I. George (John George, Jacob, Gr. Meyer), married to Catharine, daughter of Christopher Meyer, Freeburg, Pa. Removed to Ohio. See page 118.

ISSUE:

Elizabeth, married Henry Motz.

II. Lizzie (John George, Jacob, Gr. Meyer), married Frederick Richter.

III. Julia (John George, Jacob, Gr. Meyer), single.

IV. Susan (John George, Jacob, Gr. Meyer) was married to Jacob Hess; lived a short distance east of Tylersville, Sugarvalley, Clinton County, Pa. Susan staid a number of years with her uncle, Nicholas Bierly (my mother's father), of Brushvalley, while she and mother were still single.

II. Martin, m. Eva Walter. Issue: — 1. Catharine; 2. Eva; 3. Elizabeth; 4. Michael; 5. Susan; 6. Fannie; 7 John; 8. Ann.

III. Peter, m. Margaret Kreamer. Issue:—1. Mary; 2. John —gave list of families. His son, John R. Buchtel, is the founder of Buchtel College, Akron, O. 3. Mary; 4. Catharine; 5. Margaret; 6. Peter; 7. Michael; 8. Elizabeth; 9. Susan; 10. Rosanna; 11. Sallie.

IV. Solomon, m. Maria Reber. Issue:—1. Benjamin; 2. Joseph; 3. William; 4. Thomas; 5. Solomon; 6. Henry; 7. Jonathan; 8. Hannah.

V. Lucy, m. Nicholas Bierly. See note, page 66.

VI. Agnes, m. Michael Meyer. See page 82.

VII. Elizabeth, m. John George Meyer.

VIII. Catharine, m. Simon Pickle.

IX. Maria, m. Abraham Kreamer.

Mother was some older than her cousin, Susan. Mary, Susan's sister, staid at the same time out the valley with her uncle, Philip Meyer. I have not a record of Susan's children.

V. MARY (John George, Jacob, Gr. Meyer), was married to David Bottorf, Freeburg, Pa. Some of the descendants live about Freeburg.

VI. BARBARA (John George, Jacob, Gr. Meyer) was married to Jacob Haines, Freeburg, Pa. The Woodlings of Rebersburg, John and Philip, are grandchildren. A full list of Barbara's children was not procured.

VII. MARGARET (John George, Jacob, Gr. Meyer) was married to George Weaver, Pennsvalley, Pa. She died at her son-in-law's, Maj. Jerred Fisher's, Penn Hall, Pa., Sept. 17, 1882; aged 80 years, 5 months and 13 days. But there must be an error somewhere; she must either have been older or her mother must have lived later than Sept. 4, 1801, as recorded on her tombstone. See page 58. Those enumerated were children of George's first wife, Elizabeth, and the following are those of the second wife, Mary.

VIII. LYDIA (John George, Jacob, Gr. Meyer) married Benjamin Hess, Pennsvalley, Pa. The family moved West

IX. CHRISTINA (John George, Jacob, Gr. Meyer) married to John Weaver. Lived near Pine Grove Mills, Centre Co., Pa.

X. DAVID (John George, Jacob, Gr. Meyer) was married to Anna Walters.

ISSUE:

1. MARY, married to William Guss. Live at Mifflintown, Pa. (Their daughter, Carrie, visited at Rebersburg, Pa., Oct. 4, 1885).

2. Caroline, married to William Adams, Philadelphia.

3. George C. Lives at Lake, O.

4. John, Little Rock, Arkansas.

VI. Henry (son of Jacob, son of Gr. Meyer), my paternal grandfather, was married first to Mary Steese, daughter of Jacob Steese of Penns township, now Snyder County, Pa., and resided with his family near Straubsburg (Freeburg) for several years. Three of the children were born there, Henry Jacob and one — the oldest — which died in infancy. Either in 1797 or 1798 the family moved into Brushvalley, Centre County, Pa., upon a tract which had been partially cleared by John Meyer who was married to grandfather's oldest sister Catharine. See page 39. Mary Steese is said to have been a very stout and strong woman and that she had charge while still single, of a grist-mill, an occupation which on account of the rude and inconvenient construction of the mills of that age, required considerable physical strength. She died in August, 1801 of a malignant fever which was contracted while visiting with her husband her brother Frederick Steese, Snyder County (now) who was low with this fever and which he had contracted while he and his father were in Philadelphia buying goods.[1] Tradition says it was yellow fever. Grandmother was the first victim in the Valley to the dread disease, but ere long many others of the early settlers followed her. She is buried in the Lutheran and Reformed cemetery at Rebersburg. Her grave has no headstone and no one knows its exact location, but it is within a few steps of that of Philip Shott who died in 1802 of the

---

1. *Note.*—Their father also took the fever in Philadelphia and died there.

same disease, and whose grave has a tombstone with an inscription. Grandfather also took the fever and was then transported across the mountains into the east end of Pennsvalley to his sister Barbara Motz in order to receive proper care and attention. A bed was fixed upon two long poles which were fastened to the sides of two horses and in this way he was carried across the mountains by way of the old Aaronsburg road. This must have occurred about the year 1801 or 1802.

Grandfather's second wife was Margaret, daughter of John Adam Harper of Pennsvalley, who was at one time one of the associate Judges of Centre County, his term beginning in 1800. The date of the marriage I have not ascertained. Grandfather was a large man, weighing over two hundred pounds, being over six feet tall and of symmetrical build. He possessed great muscular strength and activity, and was proficient in all the athletic accomplishments of his day. Although, being of a reserved and non-aggressive disposition, he was, nevertheless, a principal in many a fierce encounter in his younger days; but it is to be hoped only in self-defence or in behalf of his friends of whom there were a legion. It is said that his brother Philip in whom the quality of meekness was not overwhelming in his earlier manhood, had, on a number of occasions to be extricated out of serious difficulties. Grandfather was well known in Centre, Snyder (now), Northumberland and other of the lower counties, in all of which he had many friends; and no doubt, not a few enemies who coveted the honor of conquering him. But he was never "knocked out." In our day a reputation of that quality is not so desirable, but in his time it was considered a proof of cowardice and consequent disgrace not to resent a real or imaginary insult by physical force. And it was the case, too, that a man's reputation as a pugilist was a standing challenge — a chip on the shoulder as it were — of which every other aspirant for like honors would feel in duty bound to take cognizance.

Grandfather was enrolled, as already stated, in some organization when but sixteen years old for the protection of the settlement against the Indians. He must have had a touch of the the martial spirit as his connection with military organizations seems to indicate. Feb. 28, 1794 he was commissioned Major of the *First Battalion 3nd Northumberland Brigade:* Jan. 4, 1802, he was commissioned Lieut. Colonel of the *131. Regt. Militia, First Brigade 10th Div.* composed of the counties of Mifflin, Huntingdon and Centre. I do not think he held any civil office except that of Justice of the Peace, commissioned Jan. 4, 1814, to succeed John Kryder who removed to Ohio about that date. Grandfather lived, as stated in another place, at the old home near Elk Creek, Brushvalley, until sometime after 1806 when he built a house on the main Brushvalley road, some twenty rods east of his son Reuben's present dwelling house. The barn which had been erected in 1806 stood still farther east and also along the main road. He was a millwright by trade, which occupation he followed a long time, but devoted his later years to farming. Among the grist-mills for which he performed the millwright work may be mentioned John Motz's mill, Woodward, Pa., erected in 1790; Tobias Pickle's mill, now owned by J. K. Meyer, Brushvalley, erected in 1801 or 1802. I do not know that grandfather enjoyed any school privileges in his youth, yet he acquired a fair education in some way. He was an assiduous reader of both German and English books and periodicals, and wrote a beautiful hand in both languages. He was a stiff Democrat and in politics had very decided opinions. He was fond of social gatherings; and as a citizen he was universally respected. He belonged to the German Reformed church and contributed liberally towards its support. Grandfather was born at Mühlbach,

Lancaster (now Lebanon) county, Oct. 15, 1764, where his folks resided until about the year 1768–1770, when they removed to Straubsburg. See page 34. He died May 17, 1820. His death was quite sudder. Returning from a trip to Jersey Shore, Pa., he caught a severe cold which resulted in Brain fever, delirium and death. He had been an affectionate husband, a kind father and had been loved with tender affection by his family, and when his wife and children, gathered round his bier to gaze upon his face for the last time, mother says, they were overwhelmed with grief and sorrow. His second wife survived him many years; she died Feb. 27, 1871, aged 83 years 7 months 27 days: both are buried in the Lutheran and Reformed cemetery at Rebersburg, Pa.

There were ten children who reached maturity; of these, it is said, Dr. Jonathan Meyer most nearly resembled his father in physical feature.

CHILDREN WITH FIRST WIFE:—

I. First child died in infancy.

II. HENRY (Henry, Jacob, Gr. Meyer), my father, was born Sept. 2, 1795; died Dec. 28, 1881; lies buried in the Lutheran and Reformed cemetery, Rebersburg, Pa., between his stepmother Margaret, and his brother Jacob. He was born near Straubsburg, Northumberland county, now Snyder county, and was two or three years old when the family moved into Brushvalley. He remained while in his minority upon his father's farm part of which he subsequently purchased and lived upon during the rest of his life. He learned the Millwright trade with his father and followed that occupation many years. Father's school privileges had been limited; consisting of a few weeks attendance during the Winter at schools which were deficient in everything except an assortment of rods to lick the scholars. However, being quite fond of reading he acquired considerable knowledge on various subjects. He read both English and German works and wrote both languages. On scriptural subjects he was well informed, being a constant reader of the Bible and other religious works. He was a member of the Evangelical church from 1830 until his decease, and did much towards the support of the Gospel, and nearly all his children belong to the same demomination. During the late war father was a War Democrat and advocated the thorough suppression of the Rebellion; but in later years he never took any decided stand in politics. August 3, 1828, he was commissioned captain of the 6th Co. 12th Regt. Pa., Militia — which I believe comprised all of his military career. Father was economical but not penurious; very plain in dress and opposed to all forms of ostentation. He disliked exceedingly to see people live beyond their means. He was quite a large man, being about six feet tall and weighing about two hundred pounds; his complexion was fair, eyes blue and hair "flax color." Father was married to Hannah, daughter of Nicholas Bierly,[1] Brushvalley, Pa. She was born May 26,

---

1. *Note.*—Melchoir Bierly, or Bherly, the ancestor of the Bierlys of Centre and Clinton Counties, Pa., came from Bavaria, some time prior to the Revolutionary War. It is thought he was married already when he emigrated. For a number of years the old couple lived with or were near neighbors to their son Anthony, on Mahantango Creek, Snyder County (now), Pa During the Indian troubles of the Revolutionary period, families fled to the lower counties for safety, and the old Bierly couple never returned. The old lady being an invalid, and the flight being sudden and in great haste, she was removed with great difficulty. There were two sons;—Nicholas, who removed to Ohio, and was seldom heard from after; and Anthony. The latter was married to Anna Maria Warner. He removed his family from the Mahantango to Brushvalley, Centre Co., Pa., about the year 1791–1792; and settled north-east of the present site of Rebersburg, Pa., about half a mile. He died April 7, 1825, aged 82 years. His wife

1800, and is at this date — January, 1890,— enjoying good health, and is still of a sound mind — in her ninetieth year.

ISSUE:—

1. MARY, married first Rev. George Weirich; second, John F. Price. She was born Jan. 30, 1824. Both husbands deceased.— *Children with first husband:*— Paulina, born May 6, 1844; married Samuel Sholl; Thomas George, born May 12, 1846; married Carrie Van Horn; Henry E., born Nov. 30,

---

was born Nov. 15, 1752; died April 3, 1841. Both are buried at Rebersburg, Pa. Anthony had twelve children; these I will name in the order of their ages as near as I can.

I. MARGARET, m. first, John Philips; 2nd, Peter Greninger.

II. NICHOLAS, died July 25, 1848, aged 73 years, 1 month and 6 days. Married to Lucy Buchtel, sister of Agnes, wife of Michael Meyer, and Elizabeth, wife of John George Meyer. See pages 58 and 59. Nicholas had ten children:—1. Nicholas, m. Catharine Mechtly; 2. Hannah, (mother) married Henry Meyer; 3. Michael, m. Mary Mallory; 4. John, m. Priscilla Wolf; 5. David, m. Magdelena Shallenbarger; 6. Anthony, m. Rachel Ruhl; 7. Reuben, m. Elizabeth Weston; 8. Peter, m. Sarah Kerstetter; 9. Simon, single; 10. George, m. Sarah Magee. All but Simon leave issue.

III. LIZZIE, m. Peter Berry.

IV. CATHARINE.

V. JOHN, born Feb. 8, 1779; died in 1870. Married Catharine Berry. Eleven children: — Christina; Elizabeth; John; Jacob; Catharine; Michael; William; Peter S.; Henry; Mary; Samuel.

VI. SARAH, m. 1st, H. Greninger, 2nd, George Lesh.

VII. EVA, m. Michael Ketner.

VIII. ROSINA, m. Christian Gramly.

IX. BARBARA, m. Frederick Womeldorf.

X. ANTHONY, died July 18, 1857, aged 67 years, 10 months and 10 days. Married Maria Crotzer. Eight children:—Melchoir; John; William; Susan; Rachel; George; Daniel; Joseph C., m. Judith Meyer.

XI. ANN, m. Philip Glantz.

XII. MARY, m. Michael Kahl.

1847; married 1st, Elmira Gramly; 2nd, Ella Whiteman; Zachariah T., born Nov. 25, 1849; married 1st, Annie Morris; 2nd, Jennie Neff.— *Children with second husband:*— Annie, born Jan. 14, 1858; died single Sept. 23, 1874; Ellen, born Oct. 25, 1856; married Isaac Rumbarger; Mary, born Oct. 30, 1859; David, born Oct. 30, 1862; married Matilda Esterline; Emma, born Jan. 1, 1865; married D. W. Mark; John, born July 1, 1867; married Annie I. Mark.

2. MATILDA, born Jan. 9, 1826; died Feb. 4, 1853, buried at St. Paul near Woodward, Pa.; married Samuel G. Mingle. He was born Nov. 30, 1821; died Aug. 14, 1884; lies buried in the Evangelical cemetery at Rebersburg, Pa. Mr. Mingle was first married to Margaret Hosterman, after her decease to Matilda as above stated, then after *her* death to her sister Catharine. Mr. Mingle lived at first at the east end of Pennsvalley, thence he removed to Rebersburg where he resided a number of years. During the latter part of his life he lived at Lock Haven with his third wife Catharine until his decease. Matilda had one child:— Susan M., born Jan. 1, 1853; married Oscar L. Kern.

3. DAVID B., born Sept. 15, 1827; married Fyetta, daughter of Anthony Bierly. He is a farmer by occupation and lives at present on a farm lying east of Jacksonville, Pa., about two miles. For many years he cultivated his father's farm. Have one child:—*Henry A.*, born Oct. 25, 1880.

4. CATHARINE, born Feb. 8, 1829; married Samuel G. Mingle who had been married to her sister Matilda, deceased. See above. Catharine lives at Lock Haven, Pa. *Children:*— Caroline E., died Nov. 2, 1863; aged 9 years, 7 months, 22 days; Effie J., born Oct. 12, 1855; Hannah M., born Dec. 26, 1858; Henry S., died June 17, 1862; aged one year.

5. DANIEL, born Feb. 24, 1831; married Matilda R. Smull in 1851. The family removed to Stephenson County, Ill., December, 1853, where they have been residing ever since, engaged in farming. Daniel had served an apprenticeship with his uncle Major John Meyer to learn the cabinet maker's trade, but followed that occupation only a few years. *Children:*— Sarah Ann. born Dec. 19, 1851; married Geo. McGilligan; Dorah Hannah, born Oct. 22, 1853; died April 7, 1854; Newton Henry, born Jan. 28, 1855; was accidentally shot Jan. 1, 1873; Thomas Ephraim, born Oct. 3, 1856; married Hilda Nelson; John Franklin, born Nov. 21, 1858; Peter David, born April 9, 1861; died Feb. 18, 1875; Emma Jane, born Oct. 22, 1863; Effie Susan, born March 9, 1866; Mary, born Aug. 11, 1868; died Sept. 20, 1868.

6. SAMUEL B., born Feb. 12, 1833; married Maggie E. Moore. His wife was born Nov. 25, 1846. Samuel lives at Milesburg, Pa., and is a millwright by occupation, having learned his trade with George Shoupe, Aaronsburg, Pa. While still single Samuel used to teach in the common schools and was considered a very successful instructor. His education was acquired in the common schools of his neighborhood,— and mainly by hard study at home without the assistance of an instructor. He also had attended the Aaronsburg Academy, Centre county, for sometime, which afforded opportunities for study in higher branches. *Children :* — Oscar J., born Feb. 7, 1864; Henry H., born March 20, 1870; Iva Alma, born Nov. 14, 1887.

7. JUDITH, born March 20, 1835; married Joseph C. Bierly. See note, page 66. The family live on a farm near Centre Mills, Pa. *Children :*—Henry Elmer, born Jan. 28, 1866; Edward S., born June 20, 1869.

8. HENRY — author of this book — was born in Miles township, Centre County, Pa., Dec. 8, 1840. It is not considered good taste for one to "blow his own horn." I shall, therefore, be very brief. I was brought up on father's farm doing such work as usually falls to the lot of farmer boys; and during the Winter season attended, two or three months in a term, the common schools of the neighborhood. In the Spring of 1860 I left home to learn the millwright trade with John Todd, then residing at Potters Mills, Pa.,— a trade which both father and grandfather had followed before me. Whatever spare time I had was generally devoted to reading, and the study of mathematics or other subjects that had a bearing on my trade. Sometime in August, 1862, I returned home and on the 19th of that month enlisted in the army for "three years or during the war." A number of my old comrades enlisted about the same time and we were a few days later organized at Camp Curtin, Harrisburg, Pa., as Company "A" of the 148. Regt. P. V. We went through the usual disciplinary stages of the volunteer soldier, and first got down to serious business at Chancellorsville, Va., May, 1863. There was in me a slight leaven of the military spirit, and the boom of cannon, the shriek of the shells, the roar of the musketry, the cheer of the Union Soldiers and the yell of the Rebels reverberating through the deep woods raised my enthusiasm to the highest pitch, and I felt as though I could myself vanquish a whole regiment of the enemy! That was while we lay on the picket line in an opposite direction and at a tolerably safe distance from the disturbance. But later on after a better acquaintance with the serious work before us, when those shrieking missiles began to come uncomfortably close and streams of mangled boys in blue came passing by us to the rear, then, well then, it must be confessed, my ardor abated very considerably. That was the mental and moral experience, I believe, of most of the soldiers. I was in

every battle in which the regiment was engaged until my discharge, among which were those of Chancellorsville, Gettysburg, Auburn Mills, Mine Run, the Wilderness and Po River or Laurel Hill, besides several skirmishes of lesser note. Never being in the hospital I took in all. I was slightly wounded at Chancellorsville, but more seriously at Po River, May 10, 1864; a minnie ball passing through my left hand near the wrist which necessitated amputation and which operation was performed May 17, 1864. by A. F. Sheldon, Surgeon in charge of Campbell Hospital, Washington, D. C. I was discharged at my own request in September following, came home and entered the Rebersburg Select School then in progress. The mutilated condition of my corporeal part rendered my trade useless to me and it became necessary to mark out a new course for the future. I taught school during the following Winter ('64 and '65), went to school again the next Summer and thus continued teaching and going to school alternately for several years. In 1866 I attended the Union Seminary, New Berlin, Pa., and in the Fall of 1868 I entered the Keystone State Normal School at Kutztown, Pa., graduating with first honors the Spring following. I assisted Supt. R. M. Magee in the Centre County Normal School for a number of years. In May, 1875, I was elected County Superintendent of Common Schools of Center Co., for a term of three years, and was re-elected without opposition to the same office May, 1878. In the Fall of 1882 I was elected a member of the State Legislature, which, for reasons that need not be stated here, was in continuous session from Jan. 2, 1883, to Dec. 6, same year. I was married at Unionville, Centre Co., Pa., Jan. 18, 1872, to Martha Jane, daughter of Thomas J. Taylor; and have lived ever since at Rebersburg, Pa. Both myself and wife joined the Evangelical Church Feb. 6, 1874. Elected Justice of the Peace Feb. 18, 1890.

Children:—Infant son, dead, Nov. 11, 1872; Hannah Jane,

born Jan. 11, 1876; Henry Taylor, born Oct. 3, 1882; Mary Matilda, born Aug. 14, 1885; Sarah Ellen, born Sept. 1, 1887; Robert William, born Aug. 14, 1889.

9. SELENA, born Oct. 28, 1844; died June 27, 1845.

III. JACOB (Henry, Jacob, Gr. Meyer) was born April 30, 1797, near Freeburg, Pa., died Aug. 19, 1873; he is buried by the side of his brother Henry (father) in the Lutheran and Reformed cemetery at Rebersburg. Jacob was never married; he lived in Brushvalley all his life, except for a brief period that he spent about Uniontown, Ohio. He had purchased a farm in Marion County, O., but through some defect in the title lost it. Jacob was not very tall, but heavy set and strong. He possessed an extraordinary memory, which he had well stored with historical facts, and an inexhaustible fund of anecdotes. In politics, he was Democratic, *very;* Reformed in religion.

IV. BENJAMIN (Henry, Jacob, Gr. Meyer) was born in Miles Township, Centre Co. (Brushvalley), where he lived during his lifetime. He was married to Mary, daughter of Melchior Poorman, who lived within a quarter of a mile of his folks. Benjamin was the youngest of the children of the first wife. He died in the early part of April, 1824, and is buried in the Lutheran and Reformed cemetery at Rebersburg. His widow was subsequently married to Benjamin Beck, also of Brushvalley.

ISSUE:

Mary, married William Aurman, Stephenson Co., Ill.

CHILDREN OF SECOND WIFE, MARGARET.

V. WILLIAM (Henry, Jacob, Gr. Meyer) was born in Miles Township, Centre Co., July 30, 1804; died of some fever, March 15, 1824; and is buried at Rebersburg. Not married.

VI. JOHN (Henry, Jacob, Gr. Meyer) was born in Miles Township, Centre Co., June 30, 1806; was first married to Mary Catharine Poorman, daughter of Daniel Poorman, who also lived near neighbor to the Meyer family. Daniel Poorman and Melchior, above mentioned, were brothers, and had emigrated from Dauphin County, Pa. John's first wife, Catharine, was a cousin of his brother Dr. Jonathan Meyer's wife, Elizabeth. His second wife's maiden name was Susan Confer. John is a cabinetmaker by trade, and has carried on this business at or near his father's old homestead all his life. He never enjoyed any educational privileges beyond those afforded by the country subscription schools of that period, and these even could not be attended regularly by pupils because of the constant demand upon their assistance for the performance of the work of the farm. Yet by assiduous reading his mind was well stored with useful knowledge on many subjects. He is a stiff Democrat—and used to take great interest in politics formerly, but was never an office-seeker himself. He was quite enthusiastic in his younger days in military matters, and held several grades of office at different periods—the last and highest being that of major. Physically he was not so fully developed as his father had been, but he was well built, strong, healthy and active, and is at this day (January 1890) still quite robust in body, and of a mind unimpaired. He was ever a faithful friend of the Meyer "clan"; and to his large fund of traditional facts on that subject the author of these pages is indebted for much valuable information.

John's first wife, Mary Catharine, was born July 9, 1816; died Oct. 22, 1849; his second wife, Susan, died in the Fall of 1858. Both are buried at Rebersburg, in the Lutheran and Reformed cemetery. John is a member of the German Reformed Church.

ISSUE WITH FIRST WIFE:

1. SARAH, born Feb. 18, 1840; married Daniel Miller, near Selinesgrove, Snyder Co., Pa.

2. ABIGAIL, born April 16, 1841; married Daniel W. Harter; live at present (1889) with her father. *Children:* —M. Kate, born Aug. 9, 1861; Rose E., born May 20, 1864; graduate of the State Normal School, Lock Haven, Pa., and is engaged in teaching; John, born Nov. 20, 1865; died June 18, 1884. (M. Kate died Feb. 9, 1890.)

3. THOMAS P., was born in Miles Township, Centre Co., Pa., Aug. 29, 1842; is married to Sadie, daughter of John and Priscilla Bierly. See note, page 66. Thomas enjoyed only the meager educational facilities which the rural districts of that period presented, but being an apt student, he advanced himself sufficiently to take charge of a public school at the age of seventeen years. He continued teaching during the Winter in the common schools of his and neighboring townships, attending the Summer sessions of the Academy, at Aaronsburg, Pa., for several years, and rapidly acquired a reputation as an efficient teacher, and made commendable progress in his studies. But when the Civil War broke out, and the Government in its dire necessity called for troops his patriotism impelled him to march in defence of his country, sacrificing all his fair prospects which the future seemed to have in store. He enlisted in August 1862 with almost a hundred of his comrades and acquaintances of

Brushvalley, Centre Co., and these were afterwards organized as company "A" of the 148 Regt., P. V. Thomas had enlisted as a private and went through all the rough experience of soldier life, performing his duties faithfully, taking part in many severe engagements among which were the battles of Chancellorsville, Gettysburg, the siege and capture of Petersburg and Richmond. He was promoted three different times, was in command for a long time of the Regimental Pioneer Corps, and during the Gettysburg and Bristoe campaigns as well as during the long siege of Petersburg he had charge of the Brigade Pioneers. During the Battle of Auburn Mills Oct. 14, 1863, Thomas with a number of others was captured, and was dependent during the following Winter upon the hospitalities dispensed by the generous officials at Libby Prison, Castle Thunder and Belle Island. But he was not fed on dainties as his attenuated appearance, when released, seemed to demonstrate. He was exchanged and returned to his regiment and served until the close of the war, receiving his discharge in June 1865. After the war he went West and spent a few years among the "cow boys" on the plains in the Texas cattle business, participating in many exhilarating adventures. "Returning East in 1872 he was elected principal of the Third Ward Schools in the city of Lock Haven, Pa., which position he held for thirteen years, when he abandoned the teacher's profession for that of Dentistry, taking a second Dental Collegiate course at the University of Maryland, Baltimore.[1] In politics Mr. Meyer is strictly Democratic, is an active worker and a man of influence in State and local politics." He is a member of the German Reformed congregation at Lock Haven, which owes its prosperous condition mainly to his liberal

---

1. *Note.* — He graduated at this old and most famous Medico-Dental College March 19, 1890.

support and untiring energy. *Children:*—Edwin J., born Nov. 24, 1874; Rose M., born March 5, 1883.

4. OLIVER PERRY, born May 29, 1844 ; died Sept. 2, 1851.

5. NATHANIEL W., born Nov. 17, 1845 ; died June 23, 1858.

6. HENRY E., born July 3, 1847 ; married to Maggie Richard, who died several years ago. Henry used to teach school formerly, but is at present engaged in some business enterprises out West. He is a man of fine physique, heavy set, strong, and seems to have inherited some of the robust qualities of his ancestors.

7. MARGARET J., born April 23, 1849 ; died Aug. 23 same year.

ISSUE WITH SECOND WIFE:

8. ELLEN, born May 25, 1855 ; married Feb. 24, 1888, to Frank H. Custard. Live at Williamsport, Pa.

VII. REUBEN (Henry, Jacob, Gr. Meyer), was born Nov. 15, 1808, on the old homestead, Brushvalley, part of which he owns at this date, while the heirs of his brother Henry own the balance of the tract. He followed farming during his life, but has retired, and now lives at Rebersburg, Pa., in the house formerly owned by Dr. Daniel J. Hilbish, deceased. He is married to Mary, daughter of George Corman. Both are members of the German Reformed Church. His wife was born July 23, 1821.

ISSUE:

1. WILLIAM C., born June 17, 1844; single. William was a soldier in the late War. He enlisted in Company "A"

148th Regt., P. V., August, 1862, and participated in a number of the sanguinary battles between the army of the Potomac and the army of Northern Virginia. Always at his post, never shirking any duty, however disagreeable or dangerous; kind and generous to his comrades in camp or on the march; cool and undaunted amidst the fiercest strife, he was a model soldier, respected by his officers, and greatly esteemed by his comrades. His coolness and seeming indifference to danger in battle was finely illustrated by an incident which occurred in the engagement at the Wheat Field —the whirlpool of the battle of Gettysburg,—on the afternoon of the second day's fight. A part of the Second Corps had been rushed forward on a "double quick" to support General Sickles, and as our regiment charged across the wheat field, and when within a few rods of the stone fence, from behind which the Confederates were pouring into us vollies, William happened to spy a rabbit in front of our line, and fired at it. It was at a moment when the uproar and din of the battle was at its highest, but he thought of the collapsed condition of his haversack, and made an effort to replenish it!

He had been slightly wounded in the brilliant charge of General Hancock into the Rebel works at Spottsylvania Court House, May 12, 1864, and was granted a short furlough. On his way home he passed through Fredericksburg, Va., where I saw him for the last time. I had reached that place a few days before, with a big hole through my left hand, near the wrist. On his return to the regiment he was killed at Deep Bottom, Va., Aug. 14, 1864, by a shell, which passed through his breast. Our infantry were lying down in line of battle as the enemy were shelling them, and William had raised himself up on his side and elbow to take a view of the field, and was struck while in that position. William was not tall, rather under the medium height, but compactly built; dark eyes and hair; and good constitution. We had always been mess-mates in the army; many a cold and dreary hour we spent together on the picket line, or trudged alongside of each other many a weary mile on the march, and we were greatly attached to each other. Now he sleeps his last long sleep in an unknown grave, in a strange country, where he fell, far from those who were near and dear to him in life.

2. JOANNA, born June 21, 1847; married Jerred B. Kreamer. The family lives at Rebersburg, Pa. *Children:*—Mary M., born Dec. 4, 1869; Gertrude S., born June 29, 1872; Ada V., born Jan. 31, 1877.

3. JEROME A., born Feb. 18, 1849; married Clara J., daughter of John Wolf, and great-granddaughter of John Nicholas Gast. See note, page 46. Jerome is living on his father's farm, which, as stated above, is a part of the tract owned by his grandfather, Henry Meyer. It may be an item of interest to some to know that there are still some "descendants" of bees on the place from a colony which grandfather brought along when he moved into the valley almost a hundred years ago. And there is an apple tree in the old orchard, near Elk Creek, on the same tract, which was also brought from Freeburg nearly a hundred years ago, measuring eleven and a half feet in circumference near its base, and still bearing fruit.

4. HENRY AMAZON, born May 29, 1851; married Theressa Snook. Lives in Sugarvalley, Clinton Co., Pa., and is a tanner by trade. *Children:* — Sallie K.; George Calvin; Henry; Reuben; Mary.

5. G. CALVIN, born Jan. 12, 1853; married Lillie Mason. Live at Pueblo, Colorado. Calvin is engaged in the mercantile business.

6. DANIEL I., born April 18, 1858; married Lizzie E. Snyder. He and Amazon live near neighbors, and follow tanning, Boonville, Clinton Co. (Sugarvalley), Pa. His wife was born May 25, 1860. *Children* :—Fredie W. S., born Dec. 9, 1883; William Cleveland, born April 22, 1885; Roy Calvin, born June 22, 1886; Emma S. V., born May 19, 1888; died April 26, 1889

7. SARAH, born Dec. 29, 1862: single; stays with her parents at Rebersburg, Pa. Sarah is a skillful performer on the organ and piano. She attended several musical institutions, among which are: Freeburg Musical College, founded and conducted by Mr. Fred. C. Meyer; Danna's Institute, O., New England Conservatory of Music, Boston.

VIII. JUDITH (Henry, Jacob, Gr. Meyer), was born Feb. 27, 1811; was married in 1838 to Philip Walker. The family lives at Clintonville, Clinton Co., Pa. Her husband died Oct. 24, 1889; he belonged to the Evangelical Association.

ISSUE:

1. ELLEN, born Oct. 16, 1838; married Lyman Eddy; live at Milesburg, Centre Co., Pa. One child, Frances, married to Calvin Zimmerman.

2. REUBEN I., born Sept. 1, 1840; died Aug. 1, 1859.

3. CYRUS M., born Nov. 23, 1842; married Lucetta Dehaas Live near Clintonville, Pa. He had been a member of Company "E." 7th Pa. Cavalry, and served two years. *Children:* —Nina B., born Oct. 14, 1869; Nellie M., born June 14, 1877; Rose., born March 3, 1884.

4. NANNIE B., born March 22, 1847; married T. S. Bell, photographer, Bellefonte, Pa.

5. **James**, born Oct. 12, 1844; died from injuries resulting from the kick of a horse, Sept. 30, 1864.

6. **Abbie**, born May 19, 1849; married Charles Dehaas. One child, Harry C., born Aug. 18, 1872. Altoona, Pa.

7. **Henry**, born Oct. 18, 1853; married Nettie Reber, Clintonville, Pa. *Children:*—Edna; Alma R., born March 13, 1885.

IX. **Susan** (Henry, Jacob, Gr. Meyer), was born Aug. 15, 1813; died Nov. 23, 1883. She was married to Griffin Rote, who was born Feb. 16, 1810; died April 24, 1879. The family used to live on a farm near Salona, Clinton Co., Pa.

ISSUE:

1. **Ellen**, born Aug. 19, 1833; died July 23, 1855. Had been married to Henry Smith.

2. **Thomas**, born Oct. 23, 1835; died Sept. 6, 1878; married to Josephine Cochenour.

3. **Cyrus W.**, born March 16, 1838; married Sade Hartman. Lives at Salona, Pa. Cyrus is a noted singer.

4. **Maggie E.**, born Oct., 1840. Single.

5. **Jettie**, born Aug. 11, 1843; married E. Blackburn; widow.

6. **Jennie**, born Nov. 7, 1847; married E. Best; West Va.

7. **Effie**, born Feb. 10, 1848; married Geo. Weymuth. Live at Lock Haven, Pa.

8. **Charles**, born Aug. 28, 1858; married Rose Chatham.

X. JONATHAN (Henry, Jacob, Gr. Meyer). Physician, was married to Elizabeth, daughter of Melchior Poorman. She was a sister of Mary, wife of Jonathan's half-brother Benjamin. Jonathan was a very skillful physician, and had an extensive practice in Sugarvalley, Clinton Co., Pa., the place of his location. In his younger days he used to teach school. He was a self-made man, and a man of more than ordinary ability; he had acquired a comprehensive knowledge of such sciences as had a direct reference to his profession, supplemented by a vast fund of general information acquired by diligent study. He read medicine with Dr. Lutz, of New Berlin, Pa., and attended the usual course of medical lectures in the Jefferson Medical College, Philadelphia. The Doctor was an uncompromising Democrat, and always took a very active part in politics, but never held any political office except once, he was elected Prothonotary of his county, serving from Dec. 1, 1858 to Dec. 1, 1861. He was of a social disposition, was kind to his family, and was idolized by his children. Physically, it is said, he greatly resembled his father. He died of apoplexy at Lock Haven, Pa., Sept. 15, 1880. His wife was born April 13, 1816; died Feb. 5, 1888; both are buried at their old home Logansville (now Loganton), Clinton Co., Pa.

ISSUE:

1. MARY JANE, born July 13, 1837; married first to John Eilert; second to Joseph Kleckner.

2. PAULINA, born Dec. 16, 1838; married first Charles H. Held; second, B. F. Kleper. Live at Boonville, Clinton Co., Pa.

3. EMMA, born Sept. 29, 1839; married Lewis Kyle, Omaha.

4. MIFFLIN R., born April 24, 1842; married at Philadel-

phia, Etta R. Hammitt. Mifflin had been a member of Co. "B", 11th Pa. Vols., late War. Resides at present in Brooklyn. *Children:*—George H., born June 21, 1881; died Jan. 18, 1887; Florence M., born Dec. 24, 1882.

5. WILLIAM F., born Jan. 3, 1844; married Oct. 28, 1866, to Emma Murray. William was a member of Co. "D", First Pa. Vol. Cavalry, late War,—and was a very gallant soldier, participating in very many hard battles. He is at present carrying on the blacksmith trade at Loganton, Clinton Co., Pa. He is a Justice of the Peace at present, and is a man of influence in his locality—and in the church (Evangelical). Physically, William is very fully developed, and possesses great strength.

6. GEORGE W., born Feb. 26, 1846; was killed Aug. 28, 1862, at the Battle of Thoroughfare Gap, Va. He had been a member of Co. "B", 11th Regt., P. V.

7. SARAH ANN, born March 27, 1848; married Nov. 10, 1865, to Robt. H. Kerstetter, Loganton, Pa.

8. JAMES M., born Aug. 20, 1850; married Chrissie Jordan.

9. HENRY HARPER, born April 5, 1852.

10. JOSEPHINE, born Oct. 12, 1854; married Wesley Reighard.

11. CHARLES O., born Aug. 18, 1856; married Lucy Kune.

XI. ABIGAIL (Henry, Jacob, Gr. Meyer), was born March 10, 1819; died of consumption, Dec. 5, 1849. Single. She used to teach school. I remember attending, when a small boy, a term she taught at Gramly's school house, Miles township, Centre Co. She is buried at Rebersburg, Pa.

VII. MICHAEL (son of Jacob, son of Gr. Meyer) was born near Mühlbach, March 20, 1765, and passed most of his youth near Straubsburg (Freeburg), whence his father had moved about the year 1768–1770. He was married to Agnes Buchtel Feb. 25, 1788 ; his wife was a sister of Elizabeth, wife of his brother John George (see page 58), and a sister also of Lucy, wife of Nicholas Bierly, (see note, page 58). Michael removed his family to Brushvalley, Centre County, Pa., in 1805 into a small cabin, which stood north-west of Rebersburg, Pa., about half a mile, and soon after built a larger house near the same spot (north a few rods), which is standing at this day, but is not habitable. He was a blacksmith by trade, an excellent mechanic, and the people of the Valley induced him to take up his abode among them by granting him some advantages in the purchase of land. There are still some carpenter's tools in the neighborhood manufactured by Michael eighty years ago, whose beautiful finish and durable qualities attest to his skill as a mechanic. Thinking that he could do better for himself and his large family in a region where land was still cheap, he removed to Stark County, Ohio, in the year 1814, and purchased a tract of nine hundred acres, paying at the rate of only one dollar and a quarter per acre. Of course it was then a wild country, and the family had to undergo many privations until the land was put in condition for cultivation and lines of communication were opened with the more civilized and improved sections of the country. Stark County was afterwards divided, and Michael's tract happened to fall into the new County—Summit—near the line. Michael erected a gristmill soon after his location in his new home, and sold it sometime after. His brothers-in-law, the Buchtels (see note, page 58), emigrated into Ohio about the same time, 1814, and several others of his Brushvalley neighbors, among whom were William Kreighbaum and John Kryder, brother of Jacob Kryder, one time one of the Associate Judges of Centre County, Pa. Michael's separation from his relatives in his native State did not sever his affection for them; it is said that he and his brother Henry were greatly attached to each other, visiting each other frequently while living near neighbors, and corresponding regularly after their separation until Henry's decease. And some of his descendants still perpetuate a sentiment of kindly regard for the memory of Henry, and have treasured in relation to him a fund of interesting anecdotes and traditions. Michael paid a visit to his friends in Pennsylvania some time after 1820; then all his brothers and sisters were dead except Philip. Michael's education seems to have been confined to a knowledge of only a few branches, but he was fond of reading, it is said, and whatever subjects he studied were thoroughly digested and assimilated. All his writing that I have seen was German, and it is likely that his reading was confined principally to the same language. He was a fine singer, an excellent violinist, and was passionately fond of music. He was a member of the German Reformed Church, and led an exemplary Christian life. Physically, he resembled his brother Philip somewhat, being broad-shouldered, heavy built, not very tall, and possessing great muscular strength. He was not of a quarrelsome disposition, and seems to have kept aloof from the broils which were so frequent in his day. Most of his children settled in the neighborhood of the old homestead in Ohio. These, I am informed, are now all dead (1889), except Philip. They leave a numerous train of descendants, who hold occasional family re-unions to keep alive the feeling of kinship, and recount the cherished traditions of their ancestors. Michael, the subject of this sketch, died Aug. 5, 1843, and was the last of his father's family to enter the "valley of the shadow of death." His wife, Agnes, was born Dec. 1, 1766; died April 23, 1852. For a list of their children I am indebted to Mrs. Amanda Steese, widow of Dr. Jocob Steese, Lake, O., and to Lewis J. Meyer, Canton, O., both descendants of Michael.

There were thirteen children, eight sons and five daughters

I. HENRY (Michael, Jacob, Gr. Meyer), born Nov. 12, 1788; died Dec. 6, 1874; was married to Elizabeth Bushong. The family lived in Ohio.

ISSUE:

1. MICHAEL; 2. HENRY; 3. JOHN; 4. ELIZABETH; 5. JONATHAN.

II. SOPHIA (Michael, Jacob, Gr. Meyer) was born Aug. 15, 1790; died Oct. 1, 1840. She was married to Ben. Pontius. Lived in Ohio.

ISSUE:

1. ELIZABETH; 2. MARY; 3. MARGARET; 4. JUDITH; 5. JOHN; 6. SUSANNA; 7. ELIZA; 8. MATILDA.

III. MICHAEL (Michael, Jacob, Gr. Meyer), born May 20, 1792; died Nov. 14, 1868; was married to Elizabeth Noll. Michael lived in Ohio. Sometime during the late War or soon after, he paid a visit to his relatives in Pennsylvania.

ISSUE:

1. LAFAYETTE; 2. WILLIAM, deceased; 3. CAROLINE.

IV. ELIZABETH (Michael, Jacob, Gr. Meyer) was born April 6, 1794; was married to Henry Buchtel, son of John, and grandson of John Buchtel, mentioned in note, page 58. Elizabeth and her husband were first cousins. The family lived in Wood County, O. There were sixteen children, one of whom is omitted from this list, it seems.

ISSUE:

1. GEORGE; 2. FANNIE; 3. LEAH; 4. RACHEL; 5. HETTIE; 6. ELIZABETH; 7. JEMIMA; 8. MELINDA; 9. MARY; 10. PASIDIA; 11. ALBERT; 12. LUCINDA; 13. SOPHIA; 14. AMANDA; 15. ESTHER, married to William Hartman,—one of their daughters is married to Cornelius, son of Anthony Bierly. See note, page 65.

V. JACOB (Michael, Jacob, Gr. Meyer) was born April 1, 1796; died ...., Huntingdon Co., Ind.; was married to Catharine Buchtel, grand-daughter of John Buchtel. See note, page 59. She is still living (1889), and is in her ninetieth year.

ISSUE:

1. PHILIP; 2. SAMUEL; 3. AGNES; 4. MARGARET; 5. JACOB; 6. ROSANNA; 7. CATHARINE; 8. LEWIS; 9. AMANDA.

VI. BARBARA (Michael, Jacob, Gr. Meyer) was born Oct. 25, 1798; died March 23, 1868; was married to John K. Bowers. She visited Centre County, Pa., about the close of the late War.

ISSUE:

1. ELIJAH; 2. ANN, married to Andrew Richards. Live in Ohio. 3. JACOB; 4. CHARLES; 5. AMANDA, married to Dr. Jacob Steese. She is a widow (1883), and lives at Lake, Ohio. To Mrs. Steese the writer is under obligations for information about her grandfather Michael's family and descendants. She and her sister, Ann (Mrs. Richards), visited relatives in Pennsylvania in 1882.

6. URIAH; 7. WILLIAM; 8. SERAPHIM.

VII. CHRISTOPHER (Michael, Jacob, Gr. Meyer) was born Nov. 10, 1800; died at Plymouth, Ind.; was married to Catharine Spade.

ISSUE:

1. ELIZA; 2. PHILIP; 3. ISAAC; 4. ELIJAH; 5. SARAH; 6. ELIZABETH.

VIII. JOSHUA (Michael, Jacob, Gr. Meyer) was born Oct. 12, 1802; died March 9, 1840. Lived in Ohio.

Issue:—SARAH.

IX. JOHN (Michael, Jacob, Gr. Meyer) was born March 23, 1805; died Feb. 27, 1872. Married first, Sarah Yearick, with whom he had six children: second, Ann Gass, with whom he had seven children. Lived in Ohio.

ISSUE—FIRST WIFE:

1. SIMON; 2. HERMAN; 3. LOUIS Y., born Oct. 20, 1836; lives in Canton, O., and is engaged in the manufacture of implements. He is the inventor of a number of implements and machines. Visited Centre Co., May, 1885, and to him the writer is also indebted for a number of facts for these pages. From him was received the statement by letter dated Nov. 6, 1889, that all his grandfather Michael's children were now deceased except Philip. He writes his name Myers. He was twice married; first, to Matilda Kreamer, July 4, 1858; second, to Hattie Cook, Jan. 25, 1874. His second wife died of typhoid fever, Sept. 19, 1889. *Children*:—Ida A.; Emma S.; Mary E.; John E.; Solomon; Sevilla; Bertha Blanche—the latter a child of the second wife. 4. HARRIET; 5. SARAH; 6. JOHN.

ISSUE WITH SECOND WIFE:

7. MARY; 8. FRANK; 9. CALVIN; 10. ELIAS; 11. MINERVA; 12. PASSIDIA; 13. Aaron.

X. MARY (Michael, Jacob, Gr. Meyer) was born March 25, 1807. Married to Samuel Spade,—Ohio.

ISSUE:

1. SUSAN; 2. SEVILLA; 3. MARGARET; 4. SARAH; 5. MATILDA; 6. HENRY; 7. NATHAN; 8. MARY ANN; 9. MELVINA; 10. AMANDA.

XI. PHILIP (Michael, Jacob, Gr. Meyer) was born Feb. 24, 1809. He and Susan were twins. Philip was married to Rosina Buchtel, grand-child of John Buchtel. See note, page 59. He paid a visit to Centre County, Pa., Oct. 7, 1885. He is the only surviving member of his father's family (1889). Lives in Ohio.

ISSUE:

1. ELIZABETH; 2. MARGARET; 3. URIAH; 4. JEFFERSON; 5. JAMES; 6. SUSAN; 7. MELINDA.

XII. SUSAN (Michael, Jacob, Gr. Meyer) was born Feb. 24, 1809; died May 23, 1824.

XIII. GEORGE (Michael, Jacob, Gr. Meyer) was born June 7, 1811; was married to Barbara Smith. Lived in Ohio.

ISSUE:

1. DAVID; 2. MARY E.; 3 REBECCA; 4. CATHARINE; 5. ELWIDA; 6. BRYSON; 7. LOUISA; 8. CHARLES; 9. AMANDA.

VIII. CHRISTOPHER (son of Jacob, son of Gr. Meyer) was younger than his brother Henry, and I think the youngest of the family. He died single, when some twenty years of age probably, from a fever of some kind, which was contracted while he and his brother Henry were doing some millwright work near the Juniata river. He returned to his father's house at Freeburg on horseback after he had been taken sick, and died in a few days. His brother Philip held him in his arms as he expired. Christopher had assisted his brother Henry (grandfather) in putting up the millwright work of John Motz's mill in 1790, Woodward, Pa.

CHRISTOPHER MEYER (son of the Meyer from Germany) was born at Mühlbach (Heidleberg township, Lancaster county, *then*) and was the youngest *son* of the family, but I am not certain that he was the youngest child as there was one daughter (if not two) and she may have been younger. Of the early life of Christopher and his brothers but little is known. Their childhood days were passed amid the stirring scenes and dangers of frontier life. The Mühlbach and the Tulpehocken witnessed not a few deadly encounters between the early settlers of that region and the hostile Indians.

Conrad Weiser, a prominent character in the early history of Pennsylvania, was their friend and near neighbor. Through his influence over the Indians and his wise diplomacy many threatened dangers from that source were averted. There is a tradition that the Meyer who came from Germany was a member of Col. Weiser's colony.

Christopher and his brother Michael left Mühlbach and purchased a tract of 700 acres near the present site of Campbellstown, Lebanon Co., Pa. It is said their father did not approve of the venture, supposing that the soil was not of much account. And it appears Michael shared his opinion as he sold out to his brother Christopher and returned to Mühlbach. This must have occurred about the year 1769 as shown by bonds of this date which Christopher and his father-in-law Alexander Schaeffer had given Michael for his interest in the tract.[1] The land, however, was of the best in

---

1. *Note.*—Christopher and Michael Meyer and Alexander Schaeffer executed bond for part of said tract to Robt. McLeary, dated April 10, 1769. In the same year, May 1st. Christopher Meyer and Alexander Schaeffer gave bond to Michael Meyer for £200. It seems Michael sold that time and returned to Mühlbach. It is said he then purchased the old Mühlbach homestead. On one of these bonds is Michael's receipt for £100, dated Aug. 12, 1771, which shows that he was then still living. Michael was never married. See page 129.

the State, and the old gentleman's opinion on the subject had been at fault. If I mistake not the tract was subsequently divided into five or six farms and apportioned among Christopher's sons. That part on which is located the old homestead is now owned by one of Christopher's grandsons. Christopher put up good substantial stone buildings on his farm modeled after the style of architecture then in vogue throughout the rural districts. I visited the place in 1883 and found the buildings still in good repair. Here Christopher remained until his decease, but all his children, except several of his grandchildren, moved to other parts. His descendants are found principally in Lebanon, Snyder and Centre Counties, Penna., and a number have moved West. It is remarkable how families migrate. Of his brother Jacob's descendants (male) not one remains, as far as I know, neither in Lebanon nor Snyder County. Christopher was married to Anna Maria, daughter of Alexander Schaeffer. See foot note, page 25. She was a sister of Catharine, wife of John Meyer of Mühlbach, who was Christopher's nephew. See page 25. "We designated," says Michael Meyer of Mühlbach, "our cousins of Campbellstown the 'big Meyers.'" A term not inappropriate as some of them were giants in stature and physical strength. For example, Michael who removed to Spring Bank, Centre Co., Pa., was a man of prodigious proportions. He weighed 386 lbs. and when passing through an ordinary door his shoulders would almost touch the sides of it. John, also, was a man of large stature, towering head and shoulders above his fellows. The descendants of Christopher, subject of this sketch, were nearly all fine singers; many of them have been, from generation to generation, instructors in music both vocal and instrumental, and have been leaders of choirs in the churches of the neighborhoods in which they resided. Honorable Jacob G. Meyer furnishes the following scrap of history illustrating this fact, which may appropriately be inserted here:—George Meyer, youngest son of Christopher and father of Hon. Jacob G., led singing in the Reformed Church, Campbellstown, Pa., from the time he was sixteen years of age (born March 25, 1782) until 1827 when he removed to Pine Creek, south of Aaronsburg, Pa. His nephew Henry Meyer, son of Michael, then conducted singing at Campbellstown until his death in 1873, and his sons now lead the choir in the same church. After George came into Pennsvalley in 1827 he conducted singing in the Reformed Church at Aaronsburg, until about the year 1832, when George, his son, took his place until 1840; then Hon. Jacob G., another son, took charge of the choir until about the year 1878, when he was succeeded by *his* son William T. Henry Meyer, Christopher's oldest son, moved into Pennsvalley, near Boalsburg, Pa., in 1823, and became the leader of the choir in the Reformed Church there, assisted by his sons Henry, Philip, Jacob and Joseph, continuing in that capacity until his decease in 1844. At present "big" Henry's sons Philip, Henry, Calvin and Jacob lead singing in the same church. Christopher Meyer, son of the subject of this sketch, settled at Freeburg, Pa., in 1800; he led singing in the church there for twenty years and his sons and grandsons ever since. His son Frederick C. is the founder and Director of the Musical College, Freeburg, an institution which has achieved merited popularity in central Pennsylvania. The Meyers of Freeburg are widely celebrated as musicians and through their zeal and efficiency in this noble profession their town has acquired a reputation as a musical centre.

Some of the Meyers were excessively fond of the chase. Grandfather Henry, several of his brothers, and Christopher's sons Michael, Jacob and George frequently visited each other at their respective homes in Penns, and Brushvalleys, and joined in the pursuit of game which was then abundant. There was no lack of dogs, and when several packs had been brought together and let loose there was sufficient music to inspire the hunters. The Mühlbach Meyers, descendants of John, were also fond of the chase.

Christopher Meyer died Aug. 2, 1801; aged 67 years. His wife Anna Maria was born Feb. 19, 1744; died Jan. 1, 1823. Both are buried in the German Reformed Cemetery, Campbellstown, Pa.

List of Children.

Henry. *See* page 92.
John. *See* page 95.
Michael. *See* page 99.
Jacob. *See* page 107.
Christopher. *See* page 109.
George. *See* page 118.
Catharine. *See* page 127.
Christina. *See* page 127.
Mary. *See* page 127.

I. HENRY (son of Christopher son of Gr. Meyer) removed from Campbellstown, Pa., where he was born and raised, to Centre County, Pa., in 1823, locating near Boalsburg, where he purchased a large tract of land. He was a man of large stature, like his son "big Henry," it is said. Some of his descendants still live at the old homestead near Boalsburg. Henry was born in 1767; died April 19, 1844. His wife, whose maiden name was Elizabeth Hurst, was born in 1779; died May 22, 1859.

There were six children, four sons and two daughters.

I. PHILIP (Henry, Christopher, Gr. Meyer) was married to Rachel Early. The couple lived near Boalsburg, Pa., on a farm. They had no children. Philip died Nov. 26, 1865.

II. JACOB (Henry, Christopher, Gr. Meyer) lived at Linden Hall, Centre Co., Pa., and was part owner of the Grist-Mill at that place. He was never married. He was born Feb. 2, 1802; died Sept. 30, 1882. I thought he greatly resembled uncle Jacob Meyer both in feature and disposition. See page 71.

III. CATHARINE (Henry, Christopher, Gr. Meyer) was born Jan. 16, 1804; died June 26, 1878. She was married to George Durst; lived at Centre Hall, Pa.

IV. HENRY (Henry, Christopher, Gr. Meyer) owned the old homestead near Boalsburg,—a farm of great fertility. He was a man of intelligence and was prominent in his section; a lover of music and a fine singer. He was a consistent member of the German Reformed Church, to which denomination his parents and all his brothers and sisters belonged I believe. On account of his large stature he was familiarly know as "big Henry Meyer." Henry was born Sept. 30, 1810; died of paralysis Oct. 5, 1888. He had been suffering for about a year. His wifes' maiden name was Catharine Hoffer; she was born March 25, 1817; died June 19, 1878. Both are buried at Boalsburg.

ISSUE:

1. MARY, born Oct. 4, 1841; married to George Kichline The family live near Pine Grove Mills, Pa. *Children:*— Mary; Sarah; Girtie.

2. ANNA, born Jan. 16, 1844; married to William Stamm. The family lives near Pine Grove Mills, Pa. *Children* (7):— Mary; Sallie; Ursinus; Jacob; Philip; Russell.

3. J. Henry, born Dec. 15, 1845; married to Martha Walker. Henry lives on a farm near Boalsburg, Pa. *Children:* — Elizabeth Blanche; Philip Bliss; Jacob Bond; Catharine Bertha; Clara Bernice; Placilla Beryl; Henry Bruce.

4. Rachel, born Aug. 8, 1847; married to Austin Dale. Resides at Lemont, Centre Co., Pa.

5. Amanda, born June 27, 1849.

6. Philip H.: born near Boalsburg, Pa., April 19, 1851; during his minority assisted his father on the farm and attended the public schools of the neighborhood in which he acquired a fair education. His father being a lover and friend of music the children were introduced to the subject at an early day, and Philip soon gave evidence of more than ordinary talent in that direction. He applied himself unremittingly during his spare moments from farm duties to the study and practice of his favorite theme, and soon acquired a reputation as an excellent musician. He attended a musical institution of Philadelphia for a brief period and of course had presented to his ready mind many suggestions which his self-discipline at home had failed to reveal to him. Beyond this he has not enjoyed the advantages afforded by higher grade institutions and his efficiency as a class instructor and skill as a performer on musical instruments are due mainly to his own unaided study and constant practice sustained by his love and natural ability for his work. At present he devotes all his time to teaching music both vocal and instrumental.

Philip is married to Sarah M. Feterolf. Lives near Boalsburg. *Children:*— Dora C.; born Nov. 16, 1884; Mary M.; born May 15, 1888; died Feb. —, 1889.

7. C. CALVIN, born July 27, 1853. Boalsburg.

8. JACOB, born May 15, 1856; married to Annie Shuey. Lives near Boalsburg. *Children:* — Catharine, Christian Calvin.

V. JOSEPH, (Henry, Christopher, Gr. Meyer), was born June 12, 1818; and was married to Beckie, daughter of George Corman, Brushvalley, Centre Co., Pa. He lived on a farm near Boalsburg. Joseph was also a musician, and acquired considerable skill as an organist in his mature years without the aid of an instructor. He died suddenly while playing the large pipe organ which was being dedicated Oct. 10, 1868, in the German Reformed Church at Boalsburg. He left no issue. His widow is married to David Sparr, Boalsburg.

VI. MARY (Henry, Christopher, Gr. Meyer), was married to John Keller. I have not ascertained the dates of her birth and death.

II. JOHN (son of Christopher son of Gr. Meyer), familiarly known as "big John", emigrated from Campbellstown to a farm near Freeburg, Pa., in 1801, a year after his brother Christopher settled there. John, as his nickname implies, was a very large man and possessed great physical strength, but was good-natured. He and his cousin Henry (grandfather) were the most prominent figures in the "racket" between the Meyers and Hartleys at Middleburg, Pa., on a certain occasion. It is said he often visited his brothers and cousins in Centre County. In his time the ties of loyalty to the 'clan' were stronger than seems to be the case now. His wife's maiden name was Esther Burkholder. He died July 17, 1842; lies buried at Freeburg.

There were ten children, six sons and four daughters.

I. J. HENRY (John, Christopher, Gr. Meyer), was born Jan. 22, 1799; was married to Barbara Trion, June 16, 1827. She was a sister of Julia, Henry's brother Jacob's wife, Henry and Jacob carried on the tanning business for a period of five years at Milroy, Mifflin County, Pa., thence removed to Centre County near the present village of Tusseyville about the year 1837. Henry's wife was born Jan. 24, 1809; died Aug. 31, 1852. Both husband and wife are buried in the cemetery of the Brick Church near Tusseyville.

ISSUE:

1. MARY A., born Nov. 9, 1829; married Henry Smith, Pine Grove Mills, Pa.

2. JOHN, born July 30, 1830; married April 10, 1854 to Catharine Keller; wife born March 16, 1833; one *child*—John Henry—live near Tusseyville.

3. FREDERICK, married Catharine Weaver; lives at Penn Hall, Pa., coach-maker; 4. HENRY, born Sept. 1836; married Elmira Bryman; lives near Tusseyville. 5. SUSAN, single, died Dec. 4, 1865, aged, 29 years 2 months 6 days. She and Henry were twins.

II. GEORGE (John, Christopher, Gr. Meyer) was born Jan. 3, 1801; died March 5, 1879. Was married to Sarah Glass. Lived at Freeburg, Pa.

ISSUE:

1. PHILIP,—had four *children*:—Martin L.; Ellen; Laura; George.

2. JOHN,—no children.

3. LEWIS,—*children*:—Wilson; Peter.

4. GEORGE,—deceased.

III. JOHN (John, Christopher, Gr. Meyer) was born in 1802. He was married first to Anna Stichter; second to Annie Kemmel. Lives at Fredonia, Mercer Co., Pa.

ISSUE:

1. JACOB,—had been a soldier in the Civil War. Six children, but names not received.

2. SAMUEL,—had also been a soldier. Four children. Both Samuel and Jacob are dead.

3. SUSAN; 4. CATHARINE; 5. LIZZIE; 6. MARY; 7. NANCY.

IV. JACOB (John, Christopher, Gr. Meyer), was born Dec. 5, 1806; died July 6, 1877; married to Julia Trion, sister of his brother Henry's wife as also of his brother Philip's wife. Jacob's wife was born March 15, 1811 and was still living during the Summer of 1888. The family lived near Tusseyville, Pennsvalley. See sketch of his brother J. Henry for several additional facts. Jacob lies buried at the Brick Church, Tusseyville.

ISSUE:

1. ESTHER, born Jan. 20, 1834; married to George Reiber, Tusseyville.

2. ELIZABETH, born April 15, 1836; married to William Boal, Tusseyville.

3. MARY ANN, born Jan. 4, 1844; married P. B. Jordan, near Tusseyville.

4. SUSANA, born Oct. 13, 1864; married to Samuel Housman, near Tusseyville.

V. MARY (John, Christopher, Gr. Meyer) was born Jan. 9, 1808; died Oct. 31, 1883; was married to Abraham Freed. Lived at Freeburg, Pa.

ISSUE:

1. JOHN; 2. ABRAHAM M.; 3. GEORGE; 4. HENRY; 5. PHILIP; 6. ELIZABETH; 7. MARY.

VI. CATHARINE (John, Christopher, Gr. Meyer), born Dec. 1, 1811; died Oct. 31, 1883. She was married to Wm. Teats.

ISSUE:

1. PHILIP; 2. LEVI; 3. ROBERT.

VII. MICHAEL (John, Christopher, Gr. Meyer) was born in 1816; he was married to Susan Arbagast. The family live at Delaware Grove, Mercer Co., Pa.

ISSUE:

1. HENRY,—had been a soldier in the late War, and was killed.

2. PHILIP,—had six children—names not reported.

3. LIZZIE,—three children—not reported.

4. JOHN; 5. GEORGE; 6. MARY ANN,—one child.

VIII. ELIZABETH (John, Christopher, Gr. Meyer) was born Aug. 5, 1817; married J. Mertz; no children.

IX. SUSAN (John, Christopher, Gr. Meyer), born June 18, 1820; married to E. Houtz, Freeburg, Pa.

ISSUE:

1. ELIZABETH; 2. MALINDA; 3. SARAH; 4. MARY; 5. RHENIE; 6. ALICE; 7. WILLIAM; 8. JOHN.

X. PHILIP (John, Christopher, Gr. Meyer), born June 12, 1823; married to Sarah Trion (or Treon), sister of Barbara and Julia, wives respectively of Philip's brothers, Henry and Jacob. Philip is engaged in the business of tanning, at Freeburg, Pa.

ISSUE:

1. JOHN L.,—one *child*:—Harry.

2. WILLIAM P.—Follows the profession of teaching. To him I am indebted for nearly all these facts in relation to his grandfather John's descendants. William had the misfortune of losing an arm through some accident, the particulars about which I have not ascertained.

3. EDWARD D.,—three *children*:—Jacob Philip, Elizabeth, Emma Jane.

4. PHILIP T.; 5. FREDERICK G.; 6. CHARLES HENRY; 7. HARVEY FRANCIS; 8. MARY, — one *child*: Verdilla; 9. ELIZABETH; 10. SARAH SUSAN.

III. MICHAEL (son of Christopher son of Gr. Meyer), was born Aug. 2, 1771; died April 1, 1842, lies buried in the Lutheran and Reformed cemetery at Rebersburg, Pa. His wife, whose maiden name was Elizabeth Derstine, was born Sept. 23, 1777, and died June 15, 1872 near State College, Pa., at her son George's home, and is buried at Boalsburg, Pa. Michael moved from Campbellstown, Lebanon County, to Spring Bank, Brushvalley, Centre Co., in the spring of 1834, where he purchased a farm. He was a man of herculean frame and strength, but of benevolent and amicable disposition. He was considerably over six feet tall and weighed 386 lbs. Several references have already been made to the subject of this sketch on other pages of this book.

There were eight children, five sons and three daughters.

I. Henry (Michael, Christopher, Gr. Meyer), was united in matrimony with Elenor, daughter of Henry Meyer and granddaughter of John Meyer and Catharine Schaeffer. See page 30. The couple were cousins as their grandmothers Anna Maria and Catharine Schaeffer were sisters. Henry was a farmer near Campbellstown, Pa. He was born Nov. 14, 1796; died Jan. 3, 1873. His wife was born Feb. 12, 1809; died Sept. 28, 1884. Both are buried in the German Reformed cemetery at Campbellstown.

ISSUE:

1. Elizabeth, born March 25, 1833; intermarried with John Horstich. Lives near Harrisburg, Pa.

2. Mary, born April 10, 1836; married to John Cassel; family lives at Harnerstown, Dauphin Co., Pa.

3. Christopher, born April 10, 1838.

4. Henry, born April 2, 1840; married Beckie Wolfersperger. Henry used to follow teaching formerly and had acquired prominence in his profession, but at present devotes his energy to farming. He owns a very nice farm near Campbellstown. To him I am under obligation for many courtesies shown me while visiting him and for information furnished for these pages.

5. John, born March 16, 1843; married Annie Hershey. Lives near Campbellstown.

6. Michael, born May 16, 1845; married to Susan Imboden. Michael owns his great-grandfather Christopher Meyer's old homestead near Campbellstown.

7. Gabriel, born April 5, 1847.

8. SAMUEL, born July 12, 1849; married to Harriet Heistand.

II. MARY (Michael, Christopher, Gr. Meyer), born May 5, 1802. She was married to Jacob Fishburn, — lived near Bellefonte, Pa.

III. MICHAEL (Michael, Christopher, Gr. Meyer), was married to Sarah Fox. Lived in Lebanon County, Pa. Michael was a man of fine physique, being six feet three inches tall, and well proportioned. He was born Feb. 10, 1804; died June 24, 1875. His wife and his brother George's were sisters.

ISSUE:

1. Infant; 2. Infant; 3. PHILIP, died at the age of 24 years; 4. ADAM, married to Annie Buser; *children:*—Eddie V.; Sallie E.; Joseph; Adam, deceased.

5. MICHAEL, married Annie Greenwalt; *children:*—Nevin, deceased; Lizzie; Michael; Sallie; Henry; Harvey.

6. LIZZIE.

7. SOLOMON, married to Amanda Breiner; *children:*—Georgie E.; Henry; Maud; Florence; Levi, deceased.

8. HENRY, married to Maggie Kreiger; *children:*—Clara E. George F.; Henry H.; Ada; Sallie May.

9. SALLIE, married to David S. Kauffman. Six children—not named.

10. GEORGE, intermarried with Emma E. Kirk; *children:*—William D.; Eaphemia.

11. JOHN, married Mary J. Rudolph; *children:*—Luther R., deceased; Mabel M.; Ralph E.

IV. GEORGE (Michael, Christopher, Gr. Meyer), was born near Campbellstown, Lebanon County, Pa., March 1, 1806. He was married to Anna Fox, who was born Feb. 24, 1806. George was a miller by trade which occupation he followed a number of years, but later in life purchased a farm near State College, Pa., and devoted his remaining days to farming. He was a man of excellent qualities, intelligent, honest, social and industrious. He labored zealously for the promotion of every good cause in his neighborhood, and the welfare of the church and the school were especially dear to his heart. In conversation he was both instructive and entertaining. Politically he was a staunch Democrat. The subject of this sketch was a member of the German Reformed Church, and exemplified his profession by a consistent Christian life. He died at his home Feb. 15, 1889, from Paralysis after a brief illness of but a few hours. He is buried at Boalsburg, Pa. His wife died March 21, 1874, and is also buried at Boalsburg.

ISSUE:—

1. JOHN HENRY, born Feb. 21, 1830; Farmer, lives west of Boalsburg, Pa., about a mile. Married to Phebe Weber. Henry is engaged in farming. From him was received considerable information in relation to his father's family. *Children:*—Anna L.; Nevin W.; George E.; Katie H.

2. ELIZABETH,—born Nov. 4, 1833. Single.

3. MARY JANE, born Nov. 1, 1835, now deceased. Married to Rev. M. A. Smith, minister of the German Reformed Church. *Children:*—Nevin, dead; Laura, dead; Bertha A.; Calvin M.; George A.; Charles M.; Mary E.; Ellen B.; Lottie J., dead.

4. CAROLINE, born July 26, 1838; died Nov. 22, 1843.

5. George, born Oct. 31, 1841 ; died Nov. 22, 1843.

6. Catharine, born Nov. 17, 1844 ; married to E. Houseman. One *child* :—Ida Minerva.

7. William Calvin, born Sept. 16, 1847 ; married first to Adaline Krumrine, with whom he had one *child*. Mary E.: married, second, Sarah A. Smeltzer.—three *children* with her : — George C.; Joseph C.; Marion B.

V. Elizabeth (Michael, Christopher, Gr. Meyer) was born Dec. 26, 1807 ; married to Felix Burkholder, now deceased. The family lived on a farm near Centre Hill, Pennsvalley, Pa. Elizabeth still living (1890). One of their children, Felix M., married to a Miss McClintic. He was formerly one of Centre County's most successful teachers, but is now engaged in selling agricultural implements.

VI. Samuel (Michael, Christopher, Gr. Meyer) was born near Campbellstown, Pa., Jan. 9, 1810 ; he was married to Elizabeth Behler, Sept. 13, 1832. His wife was born Jan. 8 1815 ; died May 21, 1867. Samuel moved from Dauphin County, Pa., in the Spring of 1833, upon a farm at Spring Bank, Brushvalley, Centre Co., Pa., and there began housekeeping. He lived in the Valley for many years, and there all his children—seventeen in number—were born. Thence he moved to Hiawatha, Kansas, but in what year I have not ascertained. Samuel is remembered by his neighbors in Brushvalley as a consistent member of the German Reformed Church ; and as a Republican in politics. No doubt he still adheres to his old convictions. March 11, 1884, I received a letter from him, enclosing a list of his children. Mr. Meyer had resided in Stephenson county, Ill., before moving to Kansas.

ISSUE:

1. PHILIP C., married to Amanda Grose. *Children:* —Samuel F.; Mary E.; George W.; Sarah J.; John H.; William C.; Ada R.; Maud I.; Corah B.; Harriet E.; Alvin B., deceased; Ammon S.

2. NANCY, — married to Daniel Hockman. *Children:* — Nathaniel, deceased; Simon J. C.; Oliver C.; Michael and Samuel, twins; Daniel; Emma L.; Nancy; Spencer; Henry; Delia.

3. MICHAEL,—married to Mary Lamy. *Children:*—Mary E.; Sarah J.; Nancy; John M.

4. ELIZABETH,—married to Samuel Machamer. *Children:* —Rose R.; Robert R.; Ralph R.

5. JOHN HENRY,—married to Louisa Sechrist. *Children:* —Samuel B.; John E.; James R.; Ida M.; Franklin U.; Daniel S.; Louisa E.; Martha M.; Sophia J., deceased; Henry H.; Ellen K.

6. PRISCILLA, — married to S. V. Meader. *Children:* —Hiram F.; George H.; Carrie B.; Artie M.; Stephen N., deceased; Phebe M.; Lulu; Julia K.

7. CATHARINE,—married to George St. Clare. *Children:* —Samuel D.; Abraham L.; Henry B.; Andrew J.; Jeanetta; William F.; Clarence G.; James; Elizabeth; two Infants dead; John; Sadie M.

8. MARY, — married Samuel Grose. Husband dead. *Children:*—Anna L.; Nancy E.; Mary E.; Ida M.; Savilla G., deceased; Lucretia D.; Orvie E.; Carrie A.

9. SARAH JANE, — married to Franklin Unangast. *Children:*—Mabel A.

10. LEAH,—married to Frank Swartz. *Children:*—Oliver F.; Arthur K.; George R., deceased; John S.; Charles E., deceased; Cyrus A.; William T.; Lena L.; Joseph G.; Clyde O.; Susan L.

11. SAMUEL and 12, RACHEL, deceased.

13. GEORGE W.,—married to Catharine Crock. *Children:* —Lula B., Lloyd F.; Infant.

14. DANIEL,—married Ettie Whitmore. No children.

15. LENO,—married to Amanda Loveland. *Children:* —Edna; Ned J.

16. HARRIET E.—

17. LUCETTA,—married to John Askey. *Children:* —Orpha E.; Ellis S.; Ernest G.

VII. CATHARINE (Michael, Christopher, Gr. Meyer), was born May 13, 1816; died Feb. 11, 1846; she was married to Daniel Dubbs, and the couple lived at Rebersburg, Pa. Mr. Dubbs, her husband, was married subsequently after Catharine's decease, to Hannah Kreamer. He died Sept. 14, 1889, aged 75 years, 11 months and 22 days. Catharine leaves no offspring. Both buried in the Lutheran and Reformed cemetery at Rebersburg, Pa.

VIII. SOLOMON (Michael, Christopher, Gr. Meyer). Born Feb. 26, 1819; died in Potter township, Pennsvalley, July 19, 1872, and is buried at Boalsburg. He was married first to Margaret Spicker, Aaronsburg, Pa., who was born Nov. 28, 1818; died Feb. 3, 1846. Second to Emeline Margaret Embich, who was born Sept. 21, 1831; died Feb. 7, 1875. In his younger days Solomon followed the profession of teaching day-school, but the natural bent of his mind was music, and he devoted the greater part of his life to teaching that subject. He was a very excellent singer himself, and as an instructor of classes in vocal music or as a conductor of singing conventions, he had but few equals. His second wife, Emaline, was also a fine singer and skillful performer on the organ and piano, and used to give instructions on those instruments. I believe all their children are musicians, some of whom have achieved considerable fame as singers and violinists. The family lived in Pennsvalley, Centre Co., Pa.

ISSUE—WITH FIRST WIFE:

1. William Franklin,—born April 15, 1841; died Dec. 21, 1843.

2. Alfred P., born July 1, 1842; married to Rebecca Early. Lives in Indiana.

3. Mary E., born Nov. 20, 1843; married to Thos. Boganrief. Lives at Mifflinburg, Pa. Mary used to follow teaching day-school.

ISSUE WITH SECOND WIFE:

4. Lowell M., born April 8, 1848; married to Annie K. Horner. Lives at Centre Hall, Pa. Lowell has had some experience in teaching classes in vocal music and conducting singing conventions. For richness and flexibility of voice, for artistic rendering of songs or any species of vocal composition he has no superior among all the musicians of his relationship.

5. Margaret E., born Nov. 28, 1849; died June 2, 1851.

6. Frederick W., born Jan. 8, 1852, married. Lives out West. Famous as a violinist.

7. LUCRETIA; 8. JOHN F.; 9. MICHAEL D.; 10. HENRY H. These four just named, deceased.

11. HARRY S., born Oct. 14, 1860; married Mary Rothermal. Lives at Williamsport, Pa.

12. LUCRETIA D., born May 20, 1865.

13. SOLOMON, born April 12, 1868.

14. EMELINE, born Dec. 24, 1869.

IV. JACOB (son of Christopher, son of Gr. Meyer) moved from Campbellstown, Pa., in March, 1828, and purchased a farm west of Millheim, Centre Co., Pa., several miles, near site of Penn Hall, where he remained until his decease, which occurred Sept. 25, 1853. He was born March 25, 1774. His wife's maiden name was Anna Sheller; she was born Dec. 25, 1775; died March 25, 1850. Jacob's occupation was farming. Reference to his fondness for the chase is made in another place in connection with several of his brothers and cousins. Michael Meyer, of Mühlbach, see page 27, remembers how, when he was a little boy, his father used to have fox-hounds sent to him in boxes by Jacob Meyer, of Pennsvalley.

There were eight children, three sons and five daughters.

I. ELIZABETH (Jacob, Christopher, Gr. Meyer), was born Feb. 26, 1801; died in 1868. Lived at Aaronsburg, Pa., for a number of years, thence moved to Centre Hall, Pa. Her husband, Henry Witmer, survived her many years. They had four children, two of whom are deceased:

1. ANNA M., married to William Wolf, merchant at Centre Hall, Pa. Mr. Wolf is a grandson of John Nicholas Gast, see note, page 46. They have one child—Witmer; who is associated with his father in the mercantile business.

2. MAGGIE, married to Isaac Smith; lives at Williamsport, Pa.; have four *children:* — Witmer, Grace, James, Clyde.

II. JACOB (Jacob, Christopher, Gr. Meyer), was born Aug. 5, 1802; died Sept. 14, 1867. Single. Lived at Penn Hall, Pa.

III. NANCY (Jacob, Christopher, Gr. Meyer), was born Sept. 14, 1804; died Sept. 23, 1886. She was married to Samuel Kryder, son of Jacob Kryder, of Pennsvalley, Pa., who was at one time one of the associate judges of Centre County, Pa. She was born at Campbellstown, Pa., and came with the family (her father's) to Pennsvalley in 1828. Her husband, who survives her, was a farmer, owning a fine tract near Cedar Springs, Clinton Co., Pa. Mrs. Kryder was an intelligent lady, and had stored up in her mind many facts in relation to the Meyer family. I visited her in 1883, and received from her some important items for this work. Her decease was quite sudden — having been ill only about wenty minutes.

ISSUE:—

1. J. CYRUS, married Sevilla Kling. Lives near Cedar Springs, Pa. Farmer. Used to teach singing classes formerly, and had acquired quite a reputation as a musician.

2. JACOB, married to Miss . .... Vonada.

3. HENRY, married to Miss ...... Best.

4. DAUGHTER,—deceased.

IV. CATHARINE (Jacob, Christopher, Gr. Meyer), was born Jan. 1, 1806. Single. Lived near Penn Hall, Pa.

V. MARY (Jacob, Christopher, Gr. Meyer), was born Dec. 7, 1807; married to Jacob Fisher, Ill.

VI. SUSAN (Jacob, Christopher, Gr. Meyer), was born Nov. 30, 1808; died Aug. 13, 1873. Single. Lived near Penn Hall, Pa.

VII. CHRISTOPHER (Jacob, Christopher, Gr. Meyer), was born in October, 1812; died June 2, 1873; was married to Mary Ann Glass. His wife was born in 1816. The family lived near Penn Hall, Pa. No children.

VIII. JOHN (Jacob, Christopher, Gr. Meyer), was born Sept. 14, 1814. Married Eleanor Smith. His wife was born Oct. 1, 1827. The family lives near Penn Hall, Pa.

ISSUE:—

1. JOHN F., deceased.

2. JACOB S., married to Susan C. Bitner. Lives on a farm near Penn Hall, Pa. During the Winter months Jacob instructs singing classes and conducts singing conventions.

V. CHRISTOPHER (son of Christopher son of Gr. Meyer) moved from Campbellstown, his native village, to Freeburg (Straubsburg *then*), Pa., about the year 1800. His brother "big" John came a year later. Christopher was married to Beckie Howeter. He was born in 1776; died June 11, 1840, aged 64 yrs. 4 mo. 20 da. His wife was born Oct. 20, 1777; died Nov. 20, 1862. A number of references have already been made to the subject of this sketch in other places and they will not be repeated. Many of his descendants are at Freeburg, Pa. There were nine childreu, four sons and five daughters.

I. FREDERICK C. (Christopher, Christopher, Gr. Meyer) was born Feb. 17, 1810; married to Mary Ann Boyer; both living at this date—Jan., 1890. Frederick is Musical Director of the Musical College at Freeburg, an institution of deserved popularity in Central Pennsylvania, and of which he is the originator. He is a very intelligent and energetic man, possessing very decided convictions in religion and politics, and his strong traits of character have left their impress upon the history of his native town and county. Formerly, for a period of forty-six years, he had been associated with his brother George C. in the mercantile business ; at present his attention is devoted almost exclusively to his Musical College. He has also been proprietor of a hotel for many years. Of the Meyer history, Frederick is full to overflowing, and to him the writer is indebted for much valuable information on the subject and for kind and courteous treatment when visiting him in 1883. Thus it will be found that his name occurs on many pages throughout this work in connection with historical facts. He is a member of the German Reformed Church Politically he is a Republican, — and he cannot understand how any Meyer could be a Democrat! Frederick can look with justifiable pride and satisfaction upon a numerous train of descendants, not one of whom would cause a fond parent's cheek to crimson with shame.

ISSUE:—

1. WILLIAM, born at Freeburg, Pa., Sept. 27, 1834; married Dec. 18, 1860, Sarah C., daughter of John A. and Amelia Hilbish of Montgomery Ferry, Perry County, Pa.; his wife was born at Liverpool, Perry Co., Pa., Mar. 2, 1837. During his youth William assisted his father about the hotel, store and farm, and attended schools of his town. From 1848 to 1853 he attended schools of a higher grade, among them being Berrysburg Classical Institute ; Select School at Selinsgrove ; Tuscarora Academy; Perrysburg Seminary and Freeburg Academy. In the interim he also acquired the art of marble cutting, working under instructions in Philadelphia in

1852. Like all the Meyer descendants of his great grandfather Christopher, William is a noted musician and has taught classes in vocal music in Dauphin, Juniata, Northumberland, Union and Centre Counties, and in almost every school district in his own County (Snyder). From 1854 to 1858 he taught in the public schools of Freeburg. In 1858 he was elected County surveyor for a term of three years, and in 1863 he was elected County Superintendent of common schools of Snyder County, and served in that capacity until 1872. He was re-elected to the same office for a fourth term in 1881. In June, 1879, Franklin and Marshall College conferred upon him the honorary degree of Master of Arts. He was appointed Notary Public in 1864; elected Justice of the Peace in 1875, and is now (1890) serving his third term. Besides the official positions above enumerated he filled a number of minor appointments of trust such as assignee, guardian, executor and administrator of estates. He has had charge of the Vocal Department in the Musical College, Freeburg, since its establishment, and is the musical conductor of its annual conventions. William is a member of the German Reformed church and has always been prominently connected with all movements in his section for the promotion of every good cause. In May, 1855, he was elected superintendent of the Lutheran and Reformed Sunday-school of his village and has filled that position now thirty-four years, representing his school in many S. School conventions in his County and his County in State Associations held in Philadelphia, Lancaster, Williamsport, Johnstown and Sunbury. He has held many positions in his church which for want of space cannot be enumerated here. It will be observed the subject of this sketch has occupied many positions of usefulness and trust in his life time, and we can pronounce no greater eulogy upon him than by saying that in all of them he acquitted himself with honor, integrity and efficiency.

Children:—Frederick C., born Sept. 24, 1861, graduate of Franklin and Marshall College; Mary A., born Feb. 9, 1863; Ida J., born July 18, 1865, m. Chas. F. Sesinger; Sarah E., born Oct. 25, 1866, died Nov. 30, 1866; Bertha B., born Nov. 8, 1870; William G., born Aug. 20, 1875; Myron A., born Apr. 23, 1878.

2. PHILIP B., born at Freeburg, Pa., Nov. 13, 1835; joined in matrimony, Dec. 6, 1861; with Sarah S., daughter of Daniel P. and Elizabeth Hilbish. The family lives at Freeburg. *Children (11)*: — Charles D., born Oct. 26, 1862; attended the Freeburg Academy, until 1879 when he entered Franklin and Marshall College, graduating from that institution in 1883, receiving the degree of Master of Arts from his Alma Mater in June, 1886. As Freshman he was chosen Prologuist of the Diagnothian Lit. Society at its public anniversary, and its anniversorian during his Senior year. In the Junior Oratorical contest, he stood next to the prize-winner. After graduation, Charles served two years creditably as Superintendent of the Public Schools of DeWitt, Iowa, and one year in like capacity in the city of Waterloo, same State. He then relinquished the profession and in 1886 entered the Columbia Law School, N. Y. City, graduating in 1887. At the May Term, same year, he was admitted to the Bar of Snyder County, Pa., and immediately located in the city of Minneapolis, Minnesota, where he has become established as an active practitioner in the State and Federal courts.—Anna Jane, born Oct. 31, 1863; has attended a number of the best musical institutions in the country, and has been teaching the subject with eminent success in a number of like institutions and higher grade schools, among which are Mrs. Abbotts' Conservatory, Phila., Millersville State Normal School; Allentown Female College; and others.—Benjamin F., born Aug. 11, 1866; died April 29, 1866; Lizzie H., born April 29, 1868; Arthur, born Sept. 20, 1870; died Feb. 11, 1885; Clement,

born Aug. 4, 1872; Mary F., born July 22, 1876; John C., born Dec. 8, 1877; Emma K., born June 2, 1879; Ella, born Apr. 8, 1881; Herbert E., born Sept. 19, 1885.

3. Caroline, married to Samuel G. Hilbish. Live near Freeburg, Pa.

4. Sarah E., married to Dr. J. C. Schaeffer. Husband dead.

5. Daniel B., was born at Freeburg, May 5, 1841; died of consumption July 7, 1874. Daniel acquired a fair education in the common schools and the Academy of Freeburg. He had entered the profession of teaching in 1860, taking charge of a school in his native village, but ill health obliged him to relinquish his work in the school-room, and he then directed his attention to other pursuits. He was an active politician, and for a number of years served as a member of the Republican Township Committee, one year as Chairman of the County Committee, and in 1872 represented Snyder County on the State Central Committee. He devoted his latter years, in connection with other pursuits, to the teaching of music. His connection with the publication of *The Freeburg Courier* is mentioned in another place, and need not be repeated here. He served as Postmaster of Freeburg from May 6, 1869, until his decease. Daniel was not married.

6. John C., deceased,—was aged about 18 years.

7. Henry B., was born July 24, 1846; was married to Elizabeth, daughter of Peter and Susan Mertz, April 5, 1875. Henry spent his boyhood days on the farm principally, and attended the public schools and the academy of his native town. He also took a business course in Bryant and

Stratton College, Harrisburg, Pa. In 1870 he became a member of the mercantile firm of G. & F. C. Moyer, succeeding them in 1887. Since 1874 he has been associated with C. F. Meyer in the publication of *The Freeburg Courier*,—of which mention will be made in another place. *Children:* —Nevin C., born Aug. 17, 1878; died Nov. 22, 1881; Ada V., born Jan. 17, 1883.

8. Lydia, married to Henry Brown. Lives at Freeburg.

9. Mary Jane,—married to F. E. Hilbish. Near Freeburg.

II. John C. (Christopher, Christopher, Gr. Meyer), was born in 1812; died Oct. 5, 1843. He was married to Catharine Hummel. (Facts from F. C. Meyer.)

ISSUE:

1. Nathaniel H., married to Catharine Yeager.

2. Emelia, married to Benjamin Rechenbach.

3. Catharine, married Peter Ocker.

III. Michael C. (Christopher, Christopher, Gr. Meyer) was born in 1814; died March 1, 1883, aged 69 years about. Joined in bonds of matrimony with Rachel Klose, a sister of Mary, wife of John Meyer. See page 119. Lived at Freeburg. (List of children received from F. C. Meyer.)

ISSUE:

1. Henry, married to Alice Hoke.

2. George K., married to Annie Hilbish.

3. Joseph C., married Catharine Straub.

4. SAMUEL, married Catharine Mains.

5. JOHN, married Lydia Meese.

6. SARAH, married Abraham Witmer.

IV. GEORGE C. (Christopher, Christopher, Gr. Meyer), was born at Freeburg, Pa., April 7, 1816. He spent his boy-hood days in his native village, acquiring in her schools a fair education for that period. From 1833 to 1841 he was engaged in the tanning business; and in 1833 he associated himself with his brother, F. C. Meyer, in the mercantile business, continuing thus associated for a period of forty-six years. Meantime his name was connected with many public enterprises of his section; and he filled many important positions in military, civil, educational and ecclesiastical affairs. He was a Major under the military organizations of his younger days; he was one of the founders of Freeburg Academy, serving thirty-four years as treasurer of the institution. He was one of the first directors of the Selinsgrove First National Bank, and has held that position for twenty-five years. March 17, 1865, he was appointed by Gov. Andrew G. Curtin Associate Judge of Snyder County to fill an unexpired term, and Oct. 8, 1886, he was elected to the same office for a full term of five years. He was Postmaster of Freeburg from July 17, 1874, until Oct. 17, 1885. Mr. Meyer is a member of the Reformed Church, and has held many important trusts in her gift, but for want of space these will not be enumerated. He is a Republican—in fact it might be stated here once for all that the Meyers of his section are all members of that party, while in Centre County they are nearly all Democrats. George was married to Eliza, daughter of John Michael and Catharine (Moor) Fisher, of Selinsgrove, Pa. His wife was born July 3, 1819. The subject of this sketch has his mind well stored with humorous anecdotes about the old Meyer stock, and many valuable traditions which have been of great service to the author of these pages.

ISSUE:

1. Calvin Fisher, was born at Freeburg, Pa., Sept. 18, 1843. He passed his younger days in his native town, attending the public schools of the place until the year 1853 when he entered Freeburg Academy, an institution founded the same year, and prosecuted for several years the study of the Classics and other preparatory branches for a collegiate course. But the idea of taking a full college course was abandoned. He entered the teacher's profession in 1862, taught five years in the common schools of Snyder, Dauphin, Schuylkill counties during the Winter terms, while during the Summer sessions, he served as teacher of the Primary Department or as assistant Principal in the Freeburg Acadamy. In 1867 he and his cousin Daniel B. Meyer purchased the *Central Courier* and removed it from Selinsgrove to Freeburg. The two were its editors and publishers until the decease of Daniel B. Meyer, the senior partner, July 7, 1874, when Daniel's brother Henry B. Meyer became associated with Calvin in the management of the paper. The name of the Journal was then changed to *The Freeburg Weekly Courier*, under which head it has been issued ever since, the subject of this sketch being its senior Editor. Calvin took a course in the Williamsport Commercial College, receiving his diploma Dec. 13, 1882. He is a gentleman of prominence in his section and has filled several positions of trust, which are so many proofs of the confidence which his many friends repose in his ability and integrity. He is recognized as a writer of more than ordinary ability, and under his management the *Courier* has become one of the prominent Journals of Central Pennsylvania. In Politics he is Republican. For some

unaccountable reason he is still single. Calvin has kindly furnished me with many items for this work, for which I am under lasting obligations.

2. Charles A., born Nov. 24, 1845; died Dec. 23, 1845.

3. James P., born Nov. 19, 1846; m. Emma Maurer.

4. George Jared, born March 24, 1850; died Sept. 16, 1852.

5. Infant daughter deceased.

6. Emeline, born Sept. 23, 1854; m. W. H. Mertz, Northumberland.

7. Amanda Catharine, born Oct. 8, 1856.

8. Sarah Emelia, born Apr. 5, 1859; m. Geo. M. Witmer; Salem, Snyder Co., Pa.

9. William Christopher, born Feb. 28, 1861.

10. Eliza Jane, born Jan. 31, 1866; died Mar. 10, 1866.

V. Susan (Christopher, Christopher, Gr. Meyer), intermarried with Gideon Klose. Date of birth of Susan and her sisters not given; I do not know, therefore, where they should be placed in the list of the family according to age.

VI. Mary (Christopher, Christopher, Gr. Meyer), married to Benjamin Armagast.

VII. Elizabeth (Christopher, Christopher, Gr. Meyer), was married to George Motz.

VIII. SARAH (Christopher, Christopher, Gr. Meyer), married first to John Motz, second to Joseph Sieber.

IX. CATHARINE (Christopher, Christopher, Gr. Meyer), was married to George Meyer son of John George Meyer, see page 59. The family moved to Ohio.—One child—Elizabeth, married to Henry Motz.

VI. GEORGE (son of Christopher, son of Gr. Meyer), was the youngest son of his father's family, and was born at Campbellstown, Lebanon Co., Pa., March 25, 1782. He came into Pennsvalley in 1827 locating on Pine creek, south of Aaronsburg, Pa., where he purchased a farm and a mill site on which a grist mill was erected. George was a man of stout physical frame and great strength, but was inferior in that respect to his giant brothers Henry, John and Michael. Elsewhere mention is made of his accomplishments as a singer. He was inordinately fond of the chase and often in company with his brother Jacob and his cousin Henry (grandfather) and others, indulged in this exhilarating pastime. His place was a recognized Head-quarters for the sporting fraternity of the neighborhood, and among those who frequently visited there, were the famous hunters of that period, the Roush brothers. George was married to his cousin, John Jacob Meyer's daughter Catharine of Pine Creek, near Jersey Shore, Pa. See page 52. She was a woman of small stature; she was of a very kind, benevolent disposition and was greatly esteemed by her friends and neighbors for her many noble qualities. She was born Dec. 2, 1788; died Mar. 13, 1858. George, her husband, died Jan. 1, 1854; both are buried in the German Reformed cemetery at Aaronsburg, Pa.

I remember accompanying my parents on a visit to the aged couple about the year 1845, and have still a faint recollection of their physical appearance. George is the only representative of his generation (second from the Germany Meyer) that I ever saw.

There were seven children, five sons and two daughters.

I. GEORGE (George, Christopher, Gr. Meyer), was born Jan. 13, 1806; joined in bonds of matrimony with Lydia Harter, who was born May 16, 1807. George was a miller by trade: lived in Pennsvalley, Pa.

ISSUE:

1. GEORGE, born Jan. 17, 1830; married to Sevilla Armagast. Was also a miller by trade, which occupation he followed for many years. At present he is the proprietor of a notion store at Coburn Station, Pa. *Children:*—William; Emma; Agnes; Edward; Tamie.

2. JULIANN, born Dec. 20, 1831; married to John Weaver.

3. MARIA, born Jan. 26, 1837; married to Jacob Ketner.

4. SAMUEL, born July 13, 1839; married Paulina Hosterman.

5. SARAH, born April 12, 1842; married Daniel Miller.

6. ANDREW, born Jan. 17, 1848; married Christina Geary. Andrew is a miller by trade. Lives near Woodward, Pennsvalley, Pa.

II. JOHN (George, Christopher, Gr. Meyer), was born Dec. 30, 1806; was married to Mary Klose, a sister of Rachel Klose, wife of Michel Meyer, Freeburg. See page 114. John lived for many years on a farm west of Rebersburg, Pa., about a mile, uear Meyer's Mill, thence he returned to Aaronsburg, Pennsvalley, Pa., where he died Jan. 28, 1878. He was a man rather below the medium height; he was of a very kindly, amiable disposition and had not an enemy in the world. He was honest and industrious, and his word was as good as a note with "approved security." His wife Mary was born April 23, 1810; died at their homestead near Rebersburg, Pa., May 26, 1865, and is buried in the Lutheran and Reformed cemetery of the latter place. John lies buried in Reformed cemetery at Aaronsburg.

ISSUE:

1. SARAH, born Dec. 25, 1838; married to Lieut. Daniel E. Shafer. Her husband had been a Lieutenant of Co. "A." 148 Regt. P. V. and died of a disease contracted in the service. Sarah lives at Aaronsburg, Pa. *Children:*—Lizzie, married Peter Shelly; Minnie.

2. JOSEPH K., born March 28, 1840; married to Mary E. Kline, who was born Aug. 23, 1845. Joseph owns the old Forster property—grist and saw-mill, Centre Mills, Brush-valley, Pa., and carries on the lumber and grain business and farming. The family are German Reformed. *Children:*—Eva, born at Loganton, Pa., Aug. 20, 1869, graduate of the Palatinate College, Meyerstown, Pa.; Flora, born near Rebersburg, Pa. April 22, 1871; John N., born Sept. 26, 1872; Sarah, born July 11, 1874; Mary E., born July 24, 1876; Hiram B., born Oct. 29, 1878; Rebecca J., born Feb. 7, 1882; Jason K., born July 20, 1885; George C., born June 13, 1887.

3. DAVID J., born July 23, 1843; married to Eliza, daughter of Daniel Kreamer. David has for many years been the proprietor and manager of the popular hotel, Centre Hall, Pa., but disposed of the property recently. German Reformed. *Children:*—Charles H., born April 26, 1866; Mary S., born September 12, 1869; John D., born August 4, 1874.

. 4. Melinda, born March 9, 1845; was married to Dr. J. Henry Zeigler of Rebersburg, Pa. Her husband died of consumption July 24, 1874.

5. Mary A., born Feb. 11, 1847.

6. George L.,—Physician—born July 18, 1849; married to Jennie Albin. Lives at Pardo, Mercer Co., Pa., where he enjoys a large and lucrative practice as a physician. *Children*:—John, born January 28, 1878; Ida; Klose; Mary; George.

7. Ellen E., born Feb. 26, 1857; married to Calvin M. Bower, Attorney-at-Law,—member of the well known legal firm, Orvis, Bower & Orvis, Bellefonte, Pa. Mr. Bower was born in Haines twp., Centre Co., Pa., April 20, 1849. The family are German Reformed; the prosperous condition of their congregation at Bellefonte is largely due to the zeal and liberality of Mr. Bower and lady.—One child,—John J., born May 9, 1875.

III. Catharine (George, Christopher, Gr. Meyer), married to Andrew Harter. Lived in Pennsvalley. She died Oct. 3, 1872; aged 64 years, 8 months, 11 days.

IV. Henry (George, Christopher, Gr. Meyer), was born July 27, 1809; died March 9, 1877. Intermarried with Elizabeth Stover. Lived on a farm south of Aaronsburg. In physical appearance Henry and his brother John could hardly be distinguished from each other. So close was the resemblance that John, it is said, on a certain occasion when away from home, seeing himself in a large mirror which extended the full length of one side of a room, imagined it was his brother, and stepped forward to shake hands, remarking, "Why, Henry, when did you come?"

ISSUE:

1. **Rebecca**, died single,—when aged about 16 years.

2. **Harriet**, married to Samuel Ard. Live near Coburn, Pennsylvania.

V. **Mary**, (George, Christopher, Gr. Meyer), married to Andrew Stover. Pennsvalley.

VI. **Philip** (George, Christopher, Gr. Meyer,) was born in Lebanon County, Pa., March 25, 1819; died June 25, 1876. Lived on Pine Creek south of Aaronsburg. He was first married to Magdalena Stover who was born near Aaronsburg, Dec. 12, 1819; died March 3, 1853. His second wife, Mary Stover, was born near Aaronsburg, April 23, 1835.

ISSUE WITH FIRST WIFE:

1. **William**, born March 15, 1842; married to Chestie, daughter of John Weaver, near Wolfe Stone, Pa. William owns and operates the grist mill west of Rebersburg about a mile. German Reformed.—*Children:*—Maggie Clara, born Jan. 4, 1870; Charles H. born Jan. 14, 1872; Early E., born Nov. 20, 1873.

2. **Catharine**; 3. **John**; 4. **Abbie**, these three died of Diphtheria about the same time and were aged respectively 21, 19 and 15 years.

5. **Jacob**, married to Susan Beam. Lives near Coburn, Pa.—*Children:*—Austin; Emelia; Cyrus.

6. **Philip** S., married first to Lillie Luckenbach, second to Annie Shall. Lives in Pennsvalley. Miller by trade. *Children:*—Warren (with first wife); with second wife: Girtie; Bessie; Orvis.

7. **Daniel**, married to Sarah Stover.—*Children:* Irvin; William.

ISSUE WITH SECOND WIFE:

8. George, died when aged about 8 years. Another child died in infancy.

9. Ellie, married to Lee Corman. Husband deceased. One child,—Warren.

10. Cyrus, married to Sarah Winkleblech.

11. Thomas.

12. Calvin.

13. Laura.

VII. Jacob G. (George, Christopher, Gr. Meyer), was born near Campbellstown, Lebanon Co., Pa., Oct. 16, 1824. He was the youngest child of the family and enjoys the distinction of being a descendant through a line of youngest sons, beginning with Christopher, son of the Meyer who came from Germany. He is one of the youngest of his generation, third from the Germany Meyer, a generation that is now (1890) almost extinct. Jacob has passed the greater part of his life near the scenes of his youth in Pennsvalley, Pa., engaged in various enterprises, and at present lives at Aaronsburg retired from active business pursuits. In his younger days he was an efficient teacher in the schools of his neighborhood, but he turned his attention principally to music both vocal and instrumental, and soon took a high stand as a skillful instructor and leader in both branches. He began to teach music when but fifteen years of age. He is the author of a number of musical compositions which are considered fine productions and have been deservedly popular. Jacob is a lover of music; all his family were musicians, and his home has for years been the Head Quarters for the musical geniuses of his neighborhood; he devoted the best days of his life to the teaching of the science in the singing-school and singing convention in his own and neighboring towns. Jacob is recognized as a man of fine intelligence, and he has exerted an amount of influence for good in the church, in education and in the numerous public questions which have from time to time come before the people for solution. He is a member of the German Reformed church, is liberal in her support and faithful to her doctrine, yet cherishing sentiments of charity towards other denominations. Politically he has always been a staunch Democrat and has ever taken an active stand in defense of his party and its principles. In the Fall of 1869 he was elected a member of the Legislature of this State (Pa.) and served very acceptably during his term of office. In private life, as well as public, Mr. Meyer bears an unblemished reputation. Temperate in his habits; unselfish in his devotion to his friends; kind and courteous to those around him; of a very sociable and gentlemanly disposition, he is a man greatly esteemed by his numerous friends and one whom it is a pleasure to meet. He is a self-made man, never having enjoyed the advantages of higher instruction except a short course at the Lewisburg Academy. In stature he is tall but not very heavy; light complextion; in voice, manner and feature he is a fair type of the Meyer tribe. Of the Meyer history he knows more than any other individual, and to him the author is indebted for much of the information contained in these pages. Mr. Meyer was married twice, first to Henrietta C. Furst, who is the mother of all of his children; she was born Nov. 21, 1825; died April 18, 1876, and lies buried in the Reformed cemetery at Aaronsburg; second to Mrs. Lydia A. Dutweiler, *nee* Strohm, who was born in Lebanon Co., Pa., May 27, 1828. Still living.

ISSUE:

1. Clara F., born Dec. 2, 1849; died Nov. 8, 1889. She

was married to W. H. Philips, merchant, Aaronsburg, Pa. One child,—Elsie, born in 1882.

2. WILLIAM T., was born near Aaronsburg, Pa., Sept. 20, 1853; married Jan. 14, 1880 to Lizzie S., daughter of John H. Musser, Aaronsburg. William attended the schools of his town which were considerably above the average grade of public schools throughout the rural districts and smaller villages, and being the fortunate possessor of a bright intellect he was enabled to rear the superstructure of a fair education, which he further developed by diligent private reading and study. But he inherited a taste for music, which was stimulated to rapid development by the atmosphere of music prevading his father's home. At the early age of eight years he began the systematic study of the science under the instructions of Prof. T. M. Carter. At ten he produced his first musical composition which was published several years later. He continued his studies under several eminent instructors successively, among whom were Dr. William Mason of New York City, one of America's most prominent Pianists, and Mr. George James Webb, celebrated Voice Teacher, of the same city. Possessing great natural talent for music; having studied under several of the best masters in the country, and having subjected himself to a persevering discipline, William became at an early age one of the most celebrated musicians of the State. After completing his course under instructors he began teaching piano and voice culture, meantime composing quite a number of piano pieces, songs, anthems, etc., some of which became very popular. A few of these are here named—space will not permit a full list:—"Freeburg Grand March," "La Tutelle" (Fantasie), "Belle Fountain", "Heavenly Musings", "Full of Life", "Moonlight in the Forest" (Nocturne), "Nigalla", 'Sound From the Ocean" (march), "The Queer Old Bachelor",

song, "Walking Down the Lane", song. His health giving way under the continuous strain upon his nervous system, William was compelled to cease giving instructions in music for a time at least, and he has been devoting his time and attention to the Notion and Fancy Goods business at Bellefonte, Pa., since April 1, 1889. *Children:*—Eva M., born July 15, 1881; Maud O., born May 15, 1886.

3. ANNIE M., born Dec. 8, 1856; married to Luther B. Stover. Live at Aaronsburg.

4. J. CALVIN, was born in Haines twp., Centre Co., Pa., south of Aaronsburg about one and a half miles, Jan. 31, 1861. He was the youngest, except an infant that lived but a few days, of a family of six children. When Calvin was but four years of age his father quit farming and moved to Aaronsburg to engage in the mercantile business, and there the subject of this sketch acquired the rudiments of an education in the public schools. Later he became a pupil of Prof. D. M. Wolf, Penn Hall, Pa., who prepared him for college In September, 1878, he entered Franklin and Marshall College, Lancaster, Pa., graduating in June, 1881, having taken the Valedictory, one of the honors of the institution. He then turned his attention to the profession of teaching, and in July, 1881, was elected assistant Principal of the public schools of Bellefonte, Pa., and in the Winter of 1883, upon the establishment of the Bellefonte High School, he was chosen Principal of that grade, being its first instructor, and graduating the first class from an institution that has grown and widened into a field of usefulness that challenges the support and confidence of the citizens of Bellefonte. In the Summer of 1884 he resigned his place as principal of the High School to take up in a more active way the study of Law. Dec. 24, 1884, after close application to

his studies in the office of Alexander and Bower, he was admitted to the Bar of Centre county. He then applied himself to the practice of Law in the office of the late Judge Adam Hoy for sêveral years, meantime taking an active part in the politics of his county, serving as chairman of the Democratic County Committee for one year. In August of 1886 he was nominated on the Democratic ticket as a candidate for District Attorney of Centre County, and was elected the following November, running far ahead of his ticket. Serving very acceptably during his term of three years he was re-elected to the same office with a greatly increased majority in the Fall of 1889. He has before him a bright future. On the 26th of May 1887, Calvin was married to Miss Lizzie H. McCalmont. One child living,—Edna Elizabeth.

VII. CATHARINE (daughter of Chistopher son of Gr. Meyer), was the oldest of the daughters—do not know whether she was the oldest child. She was married to Philip Fishburn, of Carlisle, Pa.—where the family resided. There were several daughters, one of whom is married to a Meyer at or near Carlisle,—and one son.

I. JOHN.

VIII CHRISTINA (daughter of Christopher son of Gr. Meyer), married to Samuel Carper, lived at Morris Dale, Pa. There were six children, four sons and two daughters. I. JOHN; II. FREDERICK; III. JACOB; IV. CHRISTOPHER; V. MARY; VI. CHRISTINA.

IX. MARY (daughter of Christopher son of Gr. Meyer), was married to John Adam Carper; the family lived near Linden Hall, Centre Co., Pa.—some of the descendants are residing in that neighborhood now.

There were four children, two sons and two daughters.

I. JOHN, lives near Linden Hall, Pa.; II. PHILIP, lives near State College, Pa.; III. MARY; IV. ELIZA.

Michael Meyer, one of the four sons of the Meyer who came from Germany, was never married and left no offspring. If his name were placed on the list in the order of ages it should be inserted before that of his brother Christopher as he was older. But as Michael leaves no descendants to put on record it was thought best to append a brief sketch of him here. We know very little about Michael. He was associated with his brother Christopher, and it seems Alexander Schaeffer in the purchase of a large tract of land near the present site of Campbellstown, Lebanon Co., Pa., but he sold out his interest in the tract soon after, and returned to Mühlbach, and bought, it is said, the old homestead. From old documents in my possession it appears that this occurred about the year 1769. I find his name on a receipt dated 1771 and he must have been living yet at that time. It is said he was twenty some years old when he died. He must have been older. See page 89.

Besides the four sons, John, Jacob, Michael and Christopher, the Meyer from Germany had either one or two daughters. They went south—which is all that we know about them.

GENERAL OBSERVATIONS.

The foregoing concludes the list of the descendants of the Meyer who come from the Palatinate and settled at Mühlbach carried out in some branches of the family to the fourth and fifth generation. It would have been desirable to present the record complete up to and including the fifth generation, but it would be almost impossible to secure the individual names, and the increased amount of material would have swelled this book into a large volume. It would also, have been desirable to furnish biographical sketches of a larger number of the prominent members of the family, whom, for the lack of sufficient data on hand, the author was compelled to treat with injustice by giving a mere record of their names. The Meyers belonged to that sturdy, industrious, economical and law-abiding German element which emigrated into Pennsylvania from 1700 to 1800, and which did more probably, for the material advancement and firm moral and political stability of their adopted State than any other single race. The language of the early Meyer settlers was the Pennsylvania German, a dialect brought from the Palatinate and not an American conglomerate of High German and English as some ignorantly suppose. Their mother tongue is still spoken by many even of the fifth and sixth generation, but it is now considerably changed by the influx of many English terms, and eventually the English language will supersede it entirely. The Meyers are a religious people, and among them are but few, if any, infidels. The first generations were exclusively German Reformed, and those of the present day who are residents of Lebanon, Snyder and Centre Counties, Pa., are still adhering to the same faith with a few exceptions ; while the majority of the race in the Great West belong to the Evangelical or Methodist denominations. They are firmly established in their religious beliefs, but they are neither bigoted nor superstitious. They worship the true God, but not mere creeds and images. They never nailed rusty horse-shoes above the doors of their dwellings to keep out witches! Nor were any partial to lunar or planetary signs in which to plant their potatoes,—preferring, instead, fertile soil. Politically the race is probably about equally divided. At Mühlbach, throughout Penns, Brush and Sugar Valleys, Pa., and in some sections in the West they are almost exclusively Democrats. In Snyder, Dauphin and parts of Lebanon Counties, they are principally Republican. They represent many trades and professions, but office-seeking is not a characteristic of the race. Many were mill-wrights and millers and proprietors of grist-mills. The majority, however, are farmers. Among the Meyers are not a large number that would in our time be denominated wealthy, neither are found many, if any, at the other extreme—in the poor-house. As a rule they are a temperate people, drunkards being a rare exception among them. They are law-abiding citizens; it is seldom that any indulge in litigation or stray into the criminal's cell. The older stock never took kindly to new-fangled theories, nor indulged in any ostentatious display in dress or manner but rigidly adhered to the long-tried and plain customs of their fathers. They were truly loyal to each other and ever kept bright the chain of kinship and friendship.

Finis.

LaVergne, TN USA
16 April 2010
179546LV00003B/47/P

9 781141 134540